W9-AAI-563

Chipping

The New Stock Market Method for Surviving Turbulence and Hitting a Hole-in-One

Harlan Platt, Ph.D.

Charles L. Webster Publishers
A 911Risk Inc. Company
www.ChippingStocks.com

Copyright ©2003 Harlan D Platt
Cover Photo © 2002- www.arttoday.com

Published by Charles L. Webster Publishers, a 911Risk Inc.
Company

No part of this publication may be reproduced, stored in a
retrieval system, or transmitted in any form or by any
means, electronic, mechanical, photocopying, recording,
scanning, or otherwise now known or to be invented except
as permitted under Sections 107 or 108 of the 1976 United
States Copyright Act without the prior written permission
of the Publisher, or authorization through payment of the
appropriate per-copy fee to the Copyright Clearance Center
(978) 750-8400.

This publication is designed to provide accurate and
authoritative information in regard to the subject matter
covered. It is sold with the understanding that neither the
author nor the publisher is engaged in rendering legal,
accounting, futures/security trading or other professional
service. If legal or other expert assistance is required, the
services of a competent professional person should be
sought. *From a declaration of principles jointly adopted by
a Committee of the American Bar Association and a
Committee of Publishers.*

ISBN 0-9663311-4-1

Printed in the United States of America

10 9 8 7 6 5 4 3 2 1

Dedication

To
Donald Margotta
Who Has Forgotten More About Trading than I Will Ever Know

to
Dick Omohundro and John Frabotta
Who Gave Me the Opportunity to Learn What I Know

to
Peter Stabell
Who Taught Me What I Know

and to
Michael Segal, Pierre Poulin, Henry Garelick, and Greg Fraser
Who Listened to Me While I Learned What I Know

In addition, I want thank Henry Garelick, Wes Marple, Michael Segal, Don Margotta, Greg Fraser, Moe Coyle and Peter Stabell who read an earlier draft of the manuscript. They of course bear no responsibility for its content

Table of Contents

Preface

Lets face it; the stock market has been brutal since it peaked in early 2000. Few investors have emerged unscathed from one of the longest and steadiest market declines of all times. Why did so many intelligent people lose so much money in the debacle? One reason is that most investors whole heartedly subscribed to a popular Wall Street nostrum that said markets always go up, thus invest all your funds, and never sell out. Does historical data support that approach? I don't think so. Even a naïve examination of market history refutes the underlying premise. Despite the carnage on Main Street, the stock market is here to stay. Investing will always provide opportunities to wise investors. But if traditional rules left investors vulnerable to steep market corrections, how should they invest in the future? For some investors, *Chipping: The New Stock Market Method for Surviving Turbulence and Hitting a Hole-in-One*™ may provide a better paradigm.

The market's tumble from early 2000 until mid 2002 produced horrendous losses for most investors. But the suffering was not spread around equally. Some investors actually made money. Let's see into which category you fit:

> Did you get into the market as the last upswing began and get out at the top?
> Did you get in early and never sell out?
> Did you get in at the top and sell out at the bottom? or
> Did you get in at the top and are still holding on?

The first category comprises the geniuses. They don't need this book! Instead, they should buy a great bottle of Champagne with the money and celebrate. There are not many people who belong to this group.

Most investors reside in the other three categories. Those in the second group fell for the buy-and-hold idea hook, line, and sinker. The third category is comprised of investors needing the most compassion. Buying when markets are frothing and selling during panics is a characteristic trait of ill-informed investors who succumb to Wall Street and media promotions. The final category of investors is totally confused. He doesn't know what to do next and is anxious for someone to tell him. The three losing categories of investors can benefit from a new way to invest that forces them to behave as if stock trading is a business.

Chipping provides benefits to all investors but especially those who recognize the flaws inherent in yesterday's golden investing rules. It tosses out the myth of ever-rising markets and buy-and-hold stock purchases that got investors into trouble in the first place. But don't confuse Chipping™ with day trading. Far from it, Chipping is a modern investing philosophy based partly on established finance theory and partly on practical experiences.

The investing climate won't always be dreary. Sunnier times will return. Perhaps the halcyon era of the 1990s of a nation infatuated with the stock market is gone for good. But the fundamental strength and soundness of the American economy means that U.S. equities will rise again. I wouldn't be surprised if even before this book is printed investors start to show profits on their new stock purchases.

The stock market is in our blood. How else can you explain the instant rapport between strangers who meet on an airplane or at a cocktail party and start to talk about the stock market? A comment about Wall Street's most recent plunge or spectacular rise or the name of a popular company soon has a lively group of participants engaged in conversation. And don't expect to hear a one-sided exchange. Everybody contributes by chronicling an investment story, suggesting a hot stock, or debating a new investment book or article. The only topics that may rival the magnetic attraction of the stock market are sports and sex. What is it about investing that people love? Though my training is not in anthropology, it is fairly obvious that these three activities – investing, sports, and sex – parallel the caveman's survival tasks of hunting and gathering, fighting, and procreating. Whether we acknowledge them or not, these three subconscious urges influence our behavior. The allure of investing thus combines a biological imperative to take on risk and attempt to bring down a nearby mastodon or locate enough edible plants to sustain the clan with the burgeoning need in a modern multi-functional society to put one's savings to work for the future. Investing has become an inescapable and necessary activity in contemporary life.

Society imposes a variety of obligations upon us. Some that we enjoy such as voting in elections, some that we tolerate like serving in the armed forces and some that we detest such as paying taxes. Enjoyment, toleration, and loathing also encapsulate the feelings of various people toward investing. Clearly, its appeal is not universal. For some, investing presents an exciting challenge. These souls not only perceive a need to provide their families with sustenance but they also want to be the caveman with the biggest spear. I call them *hunters*. At the other extreme are people for whom investing is onerous; a task to be avoided at any cost. I call them *bone biters*. Caveman equivalents to the modern hunter and bone biter crossed paths around a mastodon's carcass. The hunter who was responsible for the kill satisfied his family's hunger first before the bone bitter was allowed to scrap the skeleton clean. Today bone biters stake their retirement hopes on corporate pension plans and governmental programs like social security. Hunters are self-reliant; they want to earn a fortune by investing and thereby achieve financial independence.

Chipping is a book for hunters: people who perceive the stock market as an opportunity to excel and make money. She need not have much investing experience to learn from my book though it wouldn't hurt. What she does need is an open mind since this book proposes a new and exciting investment technique unlike traditional investment strategies. I call it Chipping. Chipping is a robust methodology; by which I mean that it has yielded profits on Wall Street during both bull and bear markets. Of course, no stock buying technique can earn profits when the market is in a free-fall. You should learn how to Chip and consider trying it. Chipping may help you to become a winning investor too.

My twin goals for this book are straightforward and I hope unselfish. The first is to provide an educational primer covering fundamental investment issues. The approach presents investments using a distinctly different twist: an active decision-making framework. The crux of this section is the belief that investment success comes to those who learn to evaluate choices and make decisions. Learning this framework benefits investing neophytes and journeymen alike.

Following the worst market collapse in recent memory, this message benefits most those individuals who historically did not chart their own course but rather allowed investment advisors, economic events, and popular fads to whipsaw them about. Quite possibly their investment returns have been below par. Holding these investors back, in part, is their failure to understand that investing is a systematic process that requires from them more than simply making an occasional decision to buy and sell securities or mutual funds. The investment process must include careful deliberation over a series of important decisions. Successful investors too benefit from this decision-making perspective since it may reveal flaws in their strategic thinking.

My second and preeminent goal is to introduce Chipping, a novel investment strategy. Chipping appeals to hunter investors. Chipping arms a hunter with a strategic tool that may allow him to profit whether the stock market is rising, static, or falling. Hunters should consider adopting Chipping. Bone biters, by contrast, lack the patience, free time, or psychological disposition to Chip. Yet even they gain from learning about Chipping and studying its rationale, especially if in the process they are motivated to emerge from their shell and transform themselves, albeit tepidly, into hunters by trying a few inexpensive Chips. These investors would probably have been better off had they Chipped some before the recent market crash.

I am about to upset your conception of investing fundamentals. Many investors would not have listened to my message before the markets fell apart. I hope to encourage a profound behavioral transformation among my readers but especially those of you who are bone bitters. It seems only right at this stage to tell the reader a little bit about myself. To begin with, I am an academic. That means that I make my living teaching and researching at a university. My academic affiliation frees from any dependence on Wall Street or its firms. This may help instill confidence in me as I try to unseat your preconceived ideas and beliefs. For 12 years, I served as a director on a NYSE listed mutual fund. I developed a thirst to invest in my youth (after marveling over the spectacular growth in Disney's stock price), which probably contributed to my earning a Ph.D. in economics and becoming a student of business conditions. These skills have served me well first as an economic consultant and later as a professor of finance, a corporate board member, and as an investor. Along the way I learned three basic lessons the hard way. I think every investor should know them too. You may know them already having learned them painfully yourself; hopefully, others can avoid the losses we have suffered.

The first lesson is that the stock market determines price levels by focusing not on current conditions but on the future. Some investors believe that the stock market's prescience extends out six months or longer. Readers unaware of this fact sell securities at the worst time, the bottom of the market's cycle, when things seems hopeless and buy them at the top during market euphoria. January 10, 2002 provides a perfect example of this phenomenon when the stock of Gap Inc., the clothing retailer, jumped 13% after reporting an 11% sales decline in December 2001. Bewildered investors unaware of this lesson are amazed when a stock rises after announcing bad news; wiser investors realize that the market was anticipating better times ahead for Gap Inc.

The second lesson combines two observations: 1) people are naturally optimistic and 2) over the course of history conditions do in fact improve. Invest with the knowledge that markets (not individual stocks) have a propensity to rise as labor productivity, economic profits, and prosperity increase. The final lesson, reminiscent of Horatio Alger the childhood hero, is be self-reliant. The reason for self-reliance should be obvious: no one is more interested in your success than you are.

These ideas form the intellectual motivation that led me to develop the Chipping system of investing. That philosophy has brought me Wall Street profits, though I did suffer along with everyone else in the market slide of 2002. Before Chipping, when I conformed to the "normal" investment dogma favored by Wall Street "pros", I was consistently a stock market loser. Chipping has proved to be a better paradigm, at least for me. Traditional "rules" and "conventions" don't constrain it as it focuses only on the idea of making money. Though that may sound crass, profits are the name of the game. There are benefits from learning the Chipping technique whether you ever use it or not. As a radically different trading method, it asks you to disregard rules that most investors accept without question, but in exchange it gives you a fresh perspective on Wall Street. No trading method is perfect and none is right for everybody. For that reason, I cannot guarantee that Chipping will make you rich or successful on Wall Street, but I do know that by learning the technique you will acquire something that has the potential to give you an edge in the highly competitive world of investments.

The remaining chapters fall into two sections. In the first part, comprising three chapters, a decision-making model of investments is presented. Here the reader reviews the series of decisions that are the precursors to the intelligent investment of her funds. Next a set of tools is provided that help her choose between alternative investments. These chapters provide experienced investors with a fresh look at what they are currently doing and give novices knowledge to help them begin investing.

In the second part of the book, five chapters chronicle the method of Chipping. The initial chapters explain how the method works and what the investor needs to do and not do in order to be a Chipper. A number of examples illustrate the technique. Then various strategies employed during a Chip are discussed including the idea of Chipping mutual funds. The discussion highlights some of Chipping's risks and steps investors can take to minimize them. The last chapter provides a final checklist of Chipping do's and don't. The new Chipping investor should tear these out and pin them to her computer monitor or work desk. The last chapter also speaks of Chipping Nirvana and the seven steps an investor must take in order to achieve the emotional and behavioral transformation that leads to successful Chipping. Three appendices aid the novice Chipper by providing historic examples of great stocks that presented Chipping opportunities, details on how to use the Yahoo Finance web site to obtain quick information about a company's quality, and a spreadsheet that helps investors to keep track of their stock purchases and sales.

After reading *Chipping: The New Stock Market Method for Surviving Turbulence and Hitting a Hole-in-One* and forever after always remember that investing is difficult and risky. The goal of Chipping is to reduce investment risk. Start out slowly and with a small amount of money. If you discover that you are not good at it then don't use it. But if Chipping helps you to prosper, don't let a growing sense of confidence lead you to take more risk.

Part One

The Investment Model

Chapter 1
Investing Fundamentals

ITS ALL ABOUT CHOOSING

My definition of investing begins with the word "choose" because more than anything else that is what investors do. To just get started she must choose how much (number of dollars), in what form (stocks, bonds, options, etc), where (in which country), when (timing), and with whom (which broker) to invest. Following these relatively easy preliminary decisions her choices get more difficult: picking the specific investment (which company or fund) and determining its holding period (when to sell). The dictionary tells us that the word choice means to use one's judgment to pick between alternatives. When it comes to investing there are ample opportunities to exercise judgment. For the seven questions posed above, there are nearly an infinite variety of answers to choose from. Good answers bring the investor closer to achieving her goals; bad answers keep her from realizing her goals or they consign excessive risk on her.

The dilemma of choosing is described best with the myth *The Lady and the Tiger* (by Frank Stockton) in which a young man of simple birth falls in love with a princess and is forced by her father to choose between two sealed and soundproof doors. Behind one is located the beautiful princess and a life of happiness, behind the other lies a tiger and certain death. Though the investor faces less dramatic outcomes than the young man in the story, her choices lead to equally heterogeneous outcomes–making money or losing it. The investor's future financial well-being is linked to her responses to the questions enumerated above. Many people resolve these questions through a process of rational decision-making: this book pursues that track. Other people fail to tackle these questions analytically but instead view them through personal, emotional, or cultural veils. That is a mistake. Treat every aspect of investing as if it were your business. After all, it is! There is no room when investing for emotions only careful thought and balanced reason.

Most critical amongst the investor's choices are the strategic ones involving the **type** of investments to make, the **style** of investor to be, and the holding period **behavior** to follow. But making these choices is not simple. One complication is the plethora of alternate investment strategies. The choice between strategies is almost as confusing as the selection of a new book in a large bookstore. Some strategies are classic while others are newly developed; some are easy to follow while others are hopelessly complex; some aid many investors while others help only a few. Clarity in choice comes to the investor who can articulate her goals and aspirations and is wise enough to reject strategies ill suited to meet those goals. From the remaining strategies she identifies the best approach. The appeal and advantage of any particular strategy depends on the individual's age, health, family composition, wealth, and on the economy's condition. Every investor searches for the right strategy for herself. Remember, no investment strategy works for all people at all times. As circumstances change and time passes, decisions need to be modified to meet new facts and realities.

Consider the basic investment choice between holding equities (i.e., stocks whose prices rise and fall) on the one hand and holding fixed-income securities (i.e., paying interest or dividends) on the other hand. Even if one believed that equities provide a higher return on investment than fixed-income securities, there is still a time and a place for both in most investor's lives. The choice between these types depends on the investor's current circumstances[1]. For example, she may start with equity securities at an early age when her familial obligations are fewer and then switch to fixed-income investing on short-term instruments as retirement or anticipated major expenditures such as college tuition nears. A slow-down in economic activity might move her towards a safer strategy such as fixed-income securities while indications of future economic prosperity might move her toward equities. No simple formula produces the correct investment strategy for everyone to follow since each individual has a unique allotment of inherited wealth, human capital, accumulated savings, spousal income, financial obligations, expected life span, and maybe most importantly propensity for risk. Consequently, the choice between investment strategies is an individual decision to be made personally (or by someone to whom the task is delegated) and is revisited frequently as circumstances change.

Investors make three major strategic decisions:

i.   to pursue income or growth – type of investment
ii. how much risk to tolerate – style of investing and
iii. the time period in which to hold investments – investment behavior.

The first choice between steady income and potential growth represents the most fundamental investment decision. Here investors are bifurcated into those wanting to receive either a steady flow of interest or dividends distributed regularly or to receive an uncertain though hopefully sizeable capital gain in the future. An income strategy, seeks a steady stream of income derived from a relatively stable investment portfolio. In contrast, a growth strategy aims for capital appreciation by acquiring assets

---

[1] In reality, the investor probably splits her holdings between equities and fixed-income securities and then responds to changing circumstances by altering the proportionate split between the types of securities.

whose values fluctuate. Various hybrid strategies combine elements of the two approaches to create investments that produce both income and growth though in lesser quantities.

The investor's next decision concerns the riskiness of his choices. There are a number of ways in which to measure risk. The investment world generally measures risk as volatility or likelihood that the outcome will differ from its expected value[2]. According to this definition, a riskless investment produces a constant return, whether it is income or growth, during each successive time period. You might ask the question: why would anyone want to own an investment with volatility in its returns? The answer is that volatility creates the opportunity for both gains and losses. For example, an investment in Microsoft's initial stock public offering in 1986 was a highly successful investment but it didn't go up every single day or even every quarter. Even companies with the best stock performance experience periods of rapid escalation in value followed by periods of partial retrenchment. That is, they suffer from volatility. Volatility is not necessarily a good thing but it coincides with growth in value. Too many investors during the heady 1990s bought only risky stocks because they forgot that risk and return move in tandem.

Consider your own reaction to a choice between two investments that each requires a $1 initial outlay. The first investment guarantees a $2 payoff in the future; with the second investment, at the same point in the future, you either receive just your original dollar back or you receive $3. If the two alternatives in the second investment have equal probabilities of occurring then the expected values of the two choices are equal; that is, on average you would receive an equal amount, $2.00, from either investment.

---

[2] Other risk concepts such as default risk, bankruptcy risk, or product-market risk are also studied in finance but when it comes to investments the volatility measure is the norm.

However, the second choice has risk – you might only get your $1 back or you might get $3; that is, there is volatility in its returns. Rationally you would reject the second alternative, the one with return volatility (risk), since the level of expected returns is equal in both investments. Investors require compensation in the form of higher returns for accepting more risk. If instead of the deal proposed above the second investment had an equal probability of providing either a $1 or $4 return, some investors would prefer this choice because it offers a higher expected return with some associated volatility. Other investors would stick with the first choice and its certain but lower return. The choice depends on the investor's propensity for risk and on the amount of extra return offered in exchange. That is, some investors sticking with the certain investment would accept the risky choice if the $4 return were replaced by a $5 or higher return level. There exists some higher level of return that would induce practically anyone to accept some risk. As Winston Churchill said about a totally unrelated matter, "it's only a question of price."

Investors are classified as conservative or aggressive depending on their tolerance for risk. Neither choice by itself is wrong; the right choice depends on the person, her needs and resources and her aversion to risk. The most conservative investor keeps her savings in a money-market account at the local bank. I suppose that putting money into the mattress of one's bed is even less risky – ignoring fires and robbers - but that's not investing. A somewhat less conservative investor might put some money into a certificate of deposit (i.e., a time deposit called a CD that pays a higher interest rate than a passbook account) at the bank. On the other side, the most aggressive investor employs stock options, commodity futures, or derivative contracts hoping to quickly turn a small investment into a large amount of money. These risky investments have a risk/return profile similar to those confronting a gambler in a casino. A less aggressive investor buys shares in initial public offerings (IPOs) or other high-growth potential stocks. Connecting these two sets of extreme investment strategies in terms of risk are a variety of other investments that range between plain vanilla safe strategies to highly speculative aggressive strategies. There is something for everyone in the world of investments and if there isn't Wall Street creates something new to fill the void.

Probably the most important distinction between investment strategies is how they blend risk and return together. An ultra conservative strategy matches a zero risk tolerance with miniscule returns; for example, an investment in short-term government securities. By contrast, aggressive strategies pursue substantial expected returns but in exchange accept a higher level of risk; for example, investments in equities of developing countries. The tradeoff between risk and return is the quintessential investment characteristic. But when is the amount of risk too large given the return expected from an investment? In other words, when is the investor not being adequately compensated with a higher return for accepting extra risk? To answer that question some investors rely on the Sharpe Index. The index combines risk and return into a single number[3]. It combines an individual investment's risk and return in a way that they can be compared between investments. Given a choice between two investments with

---

[3] The index is calculated by subtracting the risk-free rate of return (the interest earned on short-term government bonds from the annualized return (both income and capital growth) on an investment. This sum, called the return in excess of the risk-free rate, is then divided by the investment's risk level as measured by the standard deviation of its returns. The quotient is multiplied by 100 in order to express the ratio in unit terms. The Sharpe Index describes the amount of return received for each unit of risk. A higher index value is preferred, for example, 60 is better than 30 since for a given amount of risk twice as much excess return is earned.

equal returns, investors should choose the one with the higher Sharpe Index because that one has lower risk. Another way to think about this is that the index reveals whether the investor is earning a sufficient relative return given the amount of risk inherent in the selected investment strategy. Any investment with a lower Sharpe Index than another investment with the same amount of risk is not providing enough return to the investor to compensate for its risk.

The investor's third and final strategic decision concerns the frequency with which he modifies his holdings or investment strategies. Here investors range between active and passive. An active investor frequently adjusts his portfolio or strategy. Day trading is an extreme case of active investing. A day trader might buy and sell the same security several times during a single trading day. A passive investor, on the other hand, leaves his money in place after making an investment. This is called the buy and hold strategy. Following Berkshire Hathaway Inc.'s well-documented success with long-term investments, Warren Buffett has come to symbolize the technique of buying and holding. Mutual funds too differ in trading behavior reflected in their "turnover rate." Investors can find fund turnover rates in fund prospectuses or on their web sites.

Although the ranks of day traders swelled during the dot-com craze when the NASDAQ stock index catapulted to above 5,000, most investors remain comfortable with a buy and hold philosophy. Some passive investors seek to mirror the overall market's return (a relatively conservative strategy) by buying and holding stock-index mutual funds that replicate major market indexes such as the S&P 500. A major goal of Chipping, the investment technique that you will learn in a later chapter, is for investors to be more active and take profits. Buying stocks at the bottom, holding them as they rise, and then continuing to hold them

7

as prices fall to their old low levels is foolish. That is exactly what many investors did during the market cycle that began in early 1991 and ended in early 2000. They were passive investors and suffered as a result.

Of the three strategic decisions, the average investor is least likely to mentally debate the question of how long to hold an investment. Before buying a security most investors fail to consider under what conditions that security is to be sold. After buying it his mind jumps to other worries and concerns. These actions place him in the ranks of passive investors but not by choice only by default. A buy and hold strategy may in fact be right in terms of total returns. Yet, holding onto a security indefinitely causes him to undoubtedly miss numerous opportunities to sell it for a gain.

Certain investors never make any of the three strategic decisions. Reasons for shirking these duties include a common tendency to defer difficult decisions and an irrational fear of failure. Instead, these investors buy a stock or put money into a CD because someone else recommends the idea to them or they don't make any decisions and just leave their funds in a checking account. Bone bitters favor passive investment decision-making; they procrastinate. Hunters follow an active path, making decisions for themselves. Others recoil from a pathological fear of making a mistake. More is said about fear later in the chapters on Chipping but for now it is sufficient for every investor to know that even the best investors are not always 100% correct. George Soros lost billions on bad currency bets in 1998, Julian Robertson who ranks as a top investor lost billions of dollars and had to shut his hedge fund after shorting Internet companies too soon, and although he was known for playing baseball and not the market, Babe Ruth struck out many times. To be a winner the investor simply needs to be right more often than she is wrong. Unless strategic decisions guide an investment program, success comes to the investor only by chance or sheer luck, and that's no way to manage your money. When an investor does <u>not</u> make strategic choices for herself it means that either someone else is making them for her (which may not be a bad decision) or that she has chosen not to choose. Bone biters who have a hard time making choices are better off assigning strategic decisions to an advisor rather then not making any decisions. However, it is critical that the bone biter fully disclose to the advisor her objectives and tolerance for risk.

The investor's three strategic choices - whether to pursue income or growth, how much risk to accept, and whether to be an active or a passive investor – define the types of investments she makes and the style and behavior of the investor. A useful device to illustrate this choice-set is the tree diagram in Figure 1. In the diagram the investor's initial choice is purposefully shown as between an income and a growth strategy. This issue is the most fundamental in the investor's choice-set. A decision to pursue income means that the investor wants to receive regular interest or dividend payments; a choice to pursue growth means that the investor seeks capital appreciation. Having picked between income and growth, the investor's next choice concerns style of investing. The extreme styles are aggressive and conservative. An aggressive investor seeks out a higher level of income or a higher returning growth investment. A downside to being aggressive is increased risk. A conservative investor accepts a lower income level or a reduced growth potential in exchange for mitigating the riskiness (volatility) of his investment. Finally, with the last strategic choice the investor adopts either active or passive behavior. An active investor modifies his decisions frequently moving between various investments of the type and style he has chosen. A passive investor makes an initial set of decisions and then sticks with them.

Lets follow several of the paths in Figure 1 to see where they lead. An investor who chooses the income strategy, for example, can decide to be conservative in which case she put her money into the bank or she can be aggressive and put her funds, for

Figure 1
How the Investor Gets His Stripes

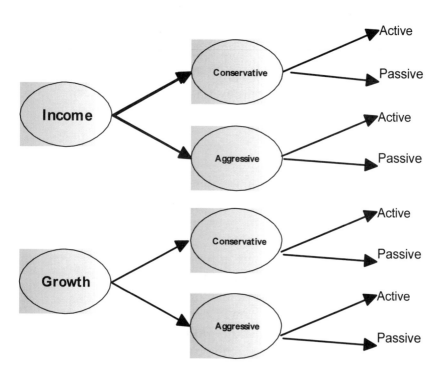

example, into a high-yield (junk) bond investment. Choosing to be an active investor means that she moves her money between banks seeking out higher interest rate offers or repeatedly buys and sells her junk bond hoping to profit on each trade. Alternatively, if she behaves passively her money stays at the original bank or she buys and holds a junk bond investment forever. By contrast, an investor who chooses the growth strategy at the outset can be conservative by investing her money, for example, in a large blue chip-consumer products company or aggressive by investing in a company promoting a hot technology. If she is an active investor she takes profits by selling her position when the price rises. If she behaves passively she puts the stock away and never sells it. Once again, there isn't a right path to follow along the tree. The investor needs to select a strategy to fit her objectives, knowledge base, and resources. While the figure looks limiting in its choice-set, the investor, in fact, has more abundant choices since she can mix and match across the tree diagram putting for example half of her funds into one category and the other half into another category.

Investment Choices and the Pursuit of Realistic Goals

The investor makes strategic choices in his pursuit of objectives regarding current income, future wealth, and financial security. Unrealistic goals cannot be met. For example, an objective of becoming a millionaire when one has little income and few savings leads a person to buy lottery tickets with his disposable cash, which is of course a bet with a very low chance of success. On the other hand, reasonable goals can be met by adopting a well-conceived investment strategy and plan. For example, the goal of accumulating enough money to put one's children through college can be met if current income is sufficient to devote a portion of each month's pay check to a college investment fund which may be income or growth oriented.

The investor's task of selecting from the catalogue of diverse investment choices is similar to a child's dilemma while visiting a candy store when she tries to decide from among the array of tantalizing options displayed before her: chewing and sucking candies, chocolates, peppermints and other tantalizing flavors galore, and colorful containers of every size. But the comparison between investors and children needs to end about here. The child allows whim and fancy to deplete her limited funds as she grabs for candies to fill her bag. The investor should be analytical and cautious. She should understand her own needs (such as putting two children through college or supporting an aged parent) and based on them should compile a realistic list of objectives (such as annually earning 5% interest or 9% capital gains on her invested capital or keeping her return volatility low). Acquiring information about each investment's properties helps her to choose wisely between them. This book provides some of the information that she needs to choose between investments.

The financial world concisely categorizes the list of potential investments into four broad groups.

- Equity securities that represent partial ownership of public companies,
- Debt securities that represent loans made to public or private companies or to governments,
- Derivative securities created as high-risk clones of other existing securities, and
- Physical assets such as buildings, racehorses, and the like,

The third and fourth cases are disregarded for the remainder of this book; the third because it describes atypical investments; the fourth because it is too idiosyncratic (your home is different than the one next door; each racehorse is a potential Kentucky Derby Winner but only one actually is, etc.). Most investors shun the third category because of its extreme risk, high degree of required sophistication, and association with the nationally publicized fiascos at Enron Corporation and Long-Term Capital Management. In contrast, most investors have the bulk of their wealth invested in the fourth category (usually their homes). Within the equity and debt security categories, the first two cases above, there are numerous investment subcategories. These are discussed in further detail below and in Chapter 2.

The investor decides how much, if any, of his funds should be allocated to each investment class. What's an investor to do? Some do nothing! The breadth of choices and the unknown consequences of decisions create an immobilizing fear of failure. Freezing up is the wrong thing to do. A number of tools exist that can help him make intelligent choices between investment classes. The two best tools are information on

- the average return earned in a particular investment category over a relatively long time period and
- the Sharpe Index to compare the risk and return profiles of alternate investment types.

First let me warn you about a hazard called the gambler's fallacy. It provides a warning that historical average returns do not provide an accurate prediction of the future. The gambler's fallacy describes an individual who increases his bet after incurring a number of consecutive losses in the belief that events eventually alternate. That is, if the roulette wheel spins nine red numbers in a row the gambler mistakenly believes that the next spin is more likely to land on a black number. In fact, the tenth spin has the same probability structure as any other spin. The operational theory of increasing your bets is probably right but the timing holds only in the long run. The danger for investors arises because the past is the past and the future is the future. Mutual fund advertisements convey this message when they say: "prior returns are no guarantee of future performance." Yet, there is value in reviewing long-term past performances. The information reveals for a variety of investment types a range of possible return outcomes that provide a basis of comparison between them. These ranges assist an investor to choose the investment category likely to meet his objectives.

The Sharpe Index, which was introduced earlier, provides an excellent way to compare the risk and return profiles of various investments. The numerator in the ratio equals the percentage difference between a specific investment's return (i.e., what it pays) and what could be earned risk free on a U.S. government security. That is, it describes what the investment gives the investor over and above what he could earn without assuming any risk. The denominator in the ratio describes the specific investment's riskiness measured by the standard deviation of returns. The quotient (i.e., the ratio itself) describes the return earned by the investor per unit of risk. A high (low) value indicates an investment that pays well (poorly) given its level of risk. The Sharpe index helps the investor choose the best investment strategy given his objectives.

The generally accepted source of information on investment returns is Ibbotson Associates in Chicago[4]. Average returns and standard deviations calculated by Ibbotson and Sharpe Indices derived by the author for the period 1926 –2000 are reported in Table 1 for large company equities (aggregated as a whole) and two broad types of bonds. The table also lists the rate of inflation during the same time span allowing real inflation-adjusted

---

[4] See *Stocks, Bonds, Bills, and Inflation: 2000 Yearbook*, Ibbotson Associates.

returns to be calculated. Several key observations emerge from the table:

- The average return on equities and fixed-income securities exceeds the rate of inflation.
- Equities and fixed-income securities are not riskless.
- Equities provide superior risk adjusted returns (the Sharpe Index) versus fixed-income securities.

These facts, based on 74 years of pre-tax data, aid investors in making the strategic decision between equities and fixed-income securities. Let see how to interpret them. From the first observation we learn that historically both equities and fixed-income securities provide the investor with a positive real rate of return; that is, they return more on average than the investor loses to inflation. The excess return over inflation is highest for equities (about 8.2% per year) and lowest for government bonds (about 2.0% per year). Also, the return on equities exceeds that from fixed-income securities by a wide margin.

Again a note of caution about the dangers of using averages to draw inferences: other data show that during periods of rapid price escalation or economic contraction that both types of investments earn a smaller differential compared to the inflation rate. During volatile periods, returns on bonds may be negative after removing inflation's impact; while equity returns may be negative even before adjusting them for inflation. Thus, do not expect, regardless of economic or political conditions, to always earn the reported 74-year average differential over the inflation rate or the reported equities premium versus fixed-income securities.

Table 1 Average Rates of Return and
Sharpe Indexes, 1926-2000

	Average Return	Standard Deviation	Sharpe Index*
Large-Company Stock	11.3%	20.1%	37.3
Long-Term Corporate Bonds	5.6%	8.7%	20.7
Long-Term Government Bond	5.1%	9.3%	14.4
Inflation	3.1%	4.5%	NR

Source: Stocks, Bonds, Bills, and Inflation: 2000 Yearbook, Ibbotson Associates.
*Based on a risk free rate of 3.8%, which is the return on US Treasury bills for the like period.

The second observation emphasizes that average returns are not constant at their 74-year averages. Equities and both types of debt securities exhibit volatility or riskiness in their returns. Not surprisingly, the riskiness of equities exceeds the volatility of bonds by a factor of more than two. The higher volatility of long-term government bonds versus corporate bonds probably surprises you. A higher standard deviation of these returns does not mean that corporations have a lower default risk than the U.S. government. Rather, the higher measured risk of government bonds is an artifact of their longer maturities (called duration) compared to corporate bonds.

The final observation is perhaps the most important. The Sharpe Index calculated for equity investments is higher (better) than the index is for bonds. The index reveals how well investors are compensated for the risk level of a particular type of investment. Comparing several Sharpe Indices identifies which investment offers a more favorable risk and return tradeoff. The indices in Table 1 suggest that equity owners, in the aggregate, receive a better total return relative to the risk of their investments than do investors in long-term government and corporate bonds. Although there are certainly times during one's life cycle or individual circumstances when it is appropriate to hold debt securities, the 74 years of data in Table 1, strongly argues that equity securities are the appropriate strategic decision for most investors at some point. Chapter 2 discusses differences between types of equity and debt securities.

Investment Styles and Holding Periods

Unlike the empirical analysis presented in the preceding section about the first strategic choice between equity and debt instruments, a more analytical approach is taken with the remaining two strategic decisions. Let me explain the difference between the two sets of decisions. The investment selection decision lends itself to empirical analysis because it is eminently sensible to compare risk and return with ratios across various investment types. On the other hand, it is not reasonable to seek specialized ratios that explain why one investor adopts a particular investment style or why another investor chooses to hold investments for a certain length of time. Investment style and holding period decisions are individual choices influenced by personality, character, and psychology. To understand these decisions and possibly yourself better, read the following sections. But don't stop there. Use this information to formulate decisions about what investment style and holding period combination work best for you.

Decisions about investment style (aggressive or conservative) and holding period behavior (active or passive) ultimately come down to personal factors. Remember, no style or holding period is right for all people at all times. Yet among clusters of investors there are behavioral similarities and common tendencies that create noteworthy commonalties. For example, aggressive investors generally are younger, male, and well to do. These are often the same people who drive their cars too fast or who climb mountains. Conservative investors are older and more self-sufficient. The image of a beachfront and a gray haired couple come to mind. Active investors lean to the younger side though both genders and all socio-economic groups fit the category. Passive investors include the old and the young and the rich and the poor. The most common combination is a passive and conservative investor.

Though it is customary to think of all investors as falling into either the conservative/passive or aggressive/active combinations, there are two other possible arrangements. Some conservative investors are active; likewise, some passive investors are aggressive. Corroboration of this unexpected assertion is found in the large number of investors who built small fortunes by investing in Internet stocks during the 1997-2000 stock bubble only to lose it because they never took any gains by selling their stock. They were aggressive and passive. No one can tell you what investing style and holding period are right for you. What I am hoping to do is to get you to see the value in making strategic decisions.

Alternative combinations of investing styles and holding periods lead to the four outcomes described taxonomically in Table 2. The droll labels I have fixed on the combinations in the table, *Thor*, *Skiing Grandma*, *Prussian General*, and *Grandpa* serve a dual purpose. First, they help the reader identify himself in the table. Second, they enhance long-term retention of the behavior each combination describes. The table also contains estimates (based on my experience) of the proportion of investors that reside in each taxonomy. As you proceed, try to answer these questions about yourselves:

    1. What quadrant in the table do you fit in?

2. What modification would change your location to an adjacent block? and
3. Where in the table should you be?

I will grade your answers below so draw circles in the diagram to mark your answers now before you read ahead. Try not to let my comic nomenclature influence the analysis of which block you belong in. Despite their derogatory labels each outcome describes some investors.

Thor was the mythological Norse god of war. Unafraid of danger he tackled any risk that stood between him and his goals. Hunters are obvious candidates for the Thor category with their aggressive investing style and active behavior. What better way to prove that you have the biggest spear than by making high-risk investments and taking profits or losses (to utilize tax advantages) at the right time? Like Thor, hunters feel no regret about having made flawed investments or profitable sales that occur below the peak price. A Thor knows that tomorrow brings another chance to do it again.

Skiing Grandma represents an anomalous investment type combining a conservative style with active behavior. What is incongruous about those choices is that so much effort is made to accomplish so little. For example, by running between banks every three months to switch her CDs to the institution paying the highest interest rate, she increases her average rate of return by perhaps ¼ of an interest rate point per year. While that behavior may generate substantial extra income depending on the investor's deposit level, an equal gain in income could probably be achieved by slightly lengthening the maturity of her CDs without having to exert much effort.

The *Prussian General* represents a military archetype whose aggressive style and passive behavior causes difficulties for this type of investor. To understand this category of investor, envision an officer who boldly advances to confront a danger but who then awaits orders from his superior officer before taking any action. A Prussian General investor invests her funds vigorously but then perversely holds on to them indefinitely and never sells whether they rise or fall. Her error is a lack of follow through. This investor knows enough to put her money to work but she does not know enough to harvest her crop.

Finally, *Grandpa* combines conservatism and passivity. This recognizable investing approach holds low-risk investments and never trades them. Despite being the dominant investing genus, based on my estimates in Table 2, its popularity is difficult to understand. This criticism holds even if Grandpa maintains a conservative equity portfolio. As seen above, over the past 74 years equity investments substantially out perform fixed-income investments. But this comparison crumbles, see Chapter 2 for details, when equity investments are stolid and poorly selected. The rapid pace of technological advancement and associated obsolescence and the short life cycles of business models argue for greater trading activism.

Some Grandpa investors are not at fault because the origin of this combination of strategic decisions was an irrevocable trust account created by a parent or grandparent or because the investor consciously decided that his current wealth is sufficient and he does not want to risk it in any way. Most investors do not fit into these defensible categories. And yet most investors are Grandpa investors; that is, their style and behavior are conservative and passive. Being a Grandpa is probably not the best decision for most investors. Being a Grandpa is fine provided that the investor consciously made that choice.

Moreover, the conservative and passive strategic combination, a Grandpa investor, faces a concealed risk: surprises and scandals that precipitate substantial overnight price changes affecting erstwhile stalwart companies. The decline in Enron's price from $80 to just pennies in a few short months will forever be a testament to this risk. To protect Grandpa against such shocks requires a substantial degree of portfolio diversification. In addition, Grandpa's strategy, by definition, never achieves stellar investment returns. Moreover, his Sharpe Index is probably very low.

Grandpa investors are not the only types facing risk. The combination of active and aggressive investing, a Thor type investor, confronts two extreme risks in pursuit of higher returns. First, success or failure may transform him into a day trader, which, in my opinion, means a gambler. Hyperactive trading seeking small fractional gains may work for a limited time but ultimately leads to disaster when a low probability event occurs or markets simply turn against the trader. A second and more common risk facing Thor is that his aggressive investing focuses on securities that are high price (though he hopes they will go higher) but low value. Poor research or limited knowledge creates this risk. Examples of this risk abound in tales told about money lost on telecommunications, Internet, and software stocks in 2001. Often these investors bought aggressive stocks because they were priced at $200 per share rather then because they were great companies or had a proven product, energetic management team, and strong finances.

Table 2's off-diagonal investor types, the Skiing Grandma and the Prussian General, are less typical combining fairly eccentric stylistic and behavioral decisions, but they still face risks similar to though in different proportion to those facing Thor and Grandpa: surprises and scandals, low returns, hyperactive trading, and high price but low value investments. But what makes

Table 2. A Taxonomy of Investing Styles and Holding Periods

	AGGRESSIVE Style	CONSERVATIVE Style
ACTIVE Holding Period	Thor: 10% of All Investors	SkiingGrandma: 5% of All Investors
PASSIVE Holding Period	Prussian General: 5% of All Investors	Grandpa: 80% of All Investors

22

Images © 2002- www.arttoday.com. Estimates of Investor Proportions Provided by the Author the Skiing Grandma and the Prussian General prototypes illogical is that they are discombobulated. The general is aggressive but unable to sell while the Grandma is willing to trade but afraid to be aggressive. The expression "it's like kissing yourself in the mirror" applies to both types; neither has much to recommend it.

Efforts to find one category that provides a comfortable level of safety and substantial returns among these four archetypes come up empty-handed. Investors need a new way to press the elements of these strategic decisions together to create a different form. That is what Chipping is about. It represents in my mind a more rational investment model that appears to be more aggressive than it actually is, if conducted properly, while being extremely active. You will learn more about it in Chapters 4 – 8.

Answering the Investor's Questions

Several pages above, you were asked to consider several questions. The first question asked you to consider where in Table 2 you fit? If during the harsh decade of the 1990s through 2002 you ultimately lost money, the reasons may be that you traded too little; i.e., your were too passive and acted like a Grandpa or a Prussian General. If the estimates provided in Table 2 are accurate, most investors should identify themselves in the Grandpa category. Yet, my survey suggests that few readers will actually put themselves there. Perhaps my estimates are incorrect. Assuming not, let me pose a few questions that may reveal your Grandpa investor tendencies.

1. Do you buy and <u>sell</u> investments regularly (include mutual funds and retirement accounts)?
2. Have you sold any investments recently?
3. When you buy an investment do you know when you will sell it?

4. Do you compare your investment returns against alternatives?
5. Do you ever make what you think is a speculative investment?
6. Are you investing in different types of securities than you were five years ago?

If you answer "NO" to all these questions you are definitely a Grandpa investor whether you think so or not! However, answering "No" to four or five questions is probably enough for you to be a Grandpa investor. Conversely, Thors answer, "YES" to all these questions, Prussian Generals answers "NO" to the first three questions, and Skiing Grandmas answer "NO" to the last three questions. In the immortal worlds of Popeye, "You yam what you yam." Unless an investor knows who he is he will have trouble improving his moneymaking prowess on Wall Street.

For my second question you considered: What modification would you need to make to change your location in the table? Given my view that off-diagonal types are dysfunctional, there are only six sensible moves for investors to make as seen in Table 3. The first four go from an off-diagonal position to one of the diagonals; the last two moves create switches along the diagonal from being a Thor to a Grandpa or vice versa. Neither diagonal position is better than the other. The choice between them is personal depending on the investor's interest in being active or aggressive. In addition to showing that it is possible to change one's strategic investment form, Table 3 also suggests that investors should avoid the dysfunctional categories and it describes the actions they can take to transform themselves should they find themselves in the wrong box.

Table 3 Required Actions to Move from One Position in Table 2 to Another

Original Position	Change	New Position
Skiing Grandma	Less Active.................	Grandpa
	Less Conservative.........	Thor
Prussian General	More Active...............	Thor
	Less Aggressive..........	Grandpa
Grandpa	More Active and More Aggressive..................	Thor
Thor	Less Active and Less Aggressive..................	Grandpa

The final question each reader considered was: Where in the table should you be? The question was a trick one because the correct answer is "none of the above." Each investor should consider moving "closer to the middle". The two non-diagonal categories are dysfunction, while the two diagonal ones are too extreme – either too cautious or too aggressive. The four categories in the table are all caricatures. They are not the only choice: an investor can blend them together. For example, a Grandpa investor who learns to take profits on occasion (adopting somewhat more active behavior) moves towards the Skiing Grandma category. While a Thor who reduces his day trading moves towards the Prussian General category. Exactly where in the grid any one investor should reside remains a highly personal decision though why anyone would choose to locate himself on the off diagonal remains a mystery to me.

ARE MUTUAL FUNDS A CHOICE?

Having made the requisite strategic decisions regarding type, style, and behavior for her investments, the next important decision is whether the investor should make investment decisions herself or through a mutual fund. At least in theory this choice is simple: the investor should choose the more profitable alternative. If she has demonstrated investment competence then she should make her own decisions. But she should let a mutual fund invest for her if it leads to better results. Mutual funds performed as poorly as individuals when market turmoil erupted in early 2001. They do not provide a safe haven from downdrafts in the market.

When comparing self-invested and mutual fund returns, relevant costs should be netted out of each. Investors often forget to deduct the cost of mutual fund loads or exit fees that are charged them at the time of original purchase or sale, respectively. Likewise, self-invested returns should be net of the cost of making investments such as time spent watching markets (in real time on the computer or at a brokers, on the TV, or in print), purchased materials, and maybe even family discord.

Despite being admonished to treat investing like a business, some people don't. A business-type decision would choose between self-investing and mutual funds based on whichever yields superior returns. But some people who aren't good investors opt to handle it themselves anyway. These are the same people who drive themselves 1,000 miles rather than board a commercial airliner or who cut their own hair. These investors enjoy the hunt. Their decision is not a problem provided that the hunter acknowledges his lower self-investing returns. Before that type of hunter would relinquish the investing reins, he would have to believe that a mutual fund could deliver vastly superior returns. Of course, some hunters are great investors who consistently beat mutual fund performance. In that case, a decision to personally orchestrate her investments is a good one.

The final decision on whether to invest on ones own or through a mutual fund is often personal. Among the reasons why some investors depend on mutual funds are that they:

- suspect that a mutual fund professional is more qualified to make investment decisions,
- lack the time or inclination to choose individual stocks or bonds,
- are unsure how to buy bonds and want to avoid the hassle of dealing with maturing bonds, and
- want to minimize bookkeeping responsibilities.

Whether they use mutual funds or buy securities themselves, investors ought to make the three strategic choices described above: to own equities or fixed-income securities, to be aggressive or conservative, and to be active or passive. Whatever their strategic decisions, investors should be able to locate a mutual fund that provides the type and style of investment that they want. With more than 7,350 stock and bond mutual funds in existence in the U.S., mutual fund investors have a nearly limitless range of investment options open to them.

Compared to owning individual stocks or bonds, mutual funds offer investors a number of advantages and disadvantages as seen in Table 4. How these elements balance out depends on the individual's degree of sophistication, wealth, and inclination to invest. For example, the first category compared in the table describes a tradeoff between commission costs a self-investor would pay against load and 12b-1 fees that a mutual fund investor incurs. Entry fees (loads) and continuing charges (12b-1 fees) are common among mutual funds. Studies show that no-load mutual funds with minimal 12b-1 fees dominate the total net return derby against high load funds[5]. On the other hand, for the small self-investing person, brokerage commissions from self-investing are generally quite high. No-load funds may have lower commission costs than self-investing brokerage costs. Wealthier investors can reduce commission costs as a percentage of total invested funds, which may lead them to prefer self-investing.

Of the many fund characteristics contrasted in Table 4, four are most responsible for convincing people to invest with mutual funds. These are diversification, security selection, reinvestment and adherence to an investment policy. The other factors in the table are more esoteric and though all investors should review them, they are probably considered by just a few. In the interest of simplicity, only the four critical items are discussed below.

Diversification is a wide-ranging concept with many alternate descriptions. The basic idea is to spread one's funds across a number of different investments. At one extreme, diversification limits investments to controlled fractions of total funds in each of several categories such as stocks, bonds, real estate, precious metals, collectibles, etc. At the other extreme, diversification is applied within investment categories such as stock or bonds. Here, for example, equity investments are spread between a number of different company's shares or if the investment is in municipal bonds across bonds of a number of different cities. Diversification reduces portfolio riskiness. Reminiscent of the medieval argument about how many angels can sit on the head of a pin, investment analysts differ regarding how many securities they think are necessary to achieve the full advantages of diversification. I don't intend to join that fray but clearly three securities are

---

[5]This point is made in an interesting research article by Wilfred Dellva and Gerard Olson in the Financial Review, " The Relationship between Mutual Fund fees and Expenses and their Effects on Performance, Vol. 33, 1988, page 85-104.

too few while 50 are probably more than enough. Of course, don't get fooled by thinking that you have diversified your portfolio when you buy stakes in 25 high tech companies, all of which produce software competing in the same niche. True diversification occurs when securities with negatively correlated rates of return are purchased[6]. An example of highly correlated returns are the prices paid to farmers for similar commodities such as wheat and corn. Droughts, consumer demand, and other variables often shock all farm prices at roughly the same time. A bank that thinks it has protected itself by diversifying its portfolio across several crops is in for big surprise in a bad weather year. On the other hand, no amount of diversification protects the investor against a general fall in the stock market, which is why it is called non-diversifiable risk.

A small investor with $10,000 of capital who diversifies by spreading her funds between the equities of 25 companies would have only $400 to invest per firm on average. Small equity investments by themselves are not bad but they result in disproportionately high commission costs and require an inordinate level of research in order to

---

[6] This is called Markowitz diversification. For example, General Motor's stock would be negatively correlation with the stock of a bus company or a rail passenger company. Movement of consumers from bus travel, for example, to automobiles would depress the bus company stock and raise the car company's stock thereby creating negatively correlated returns.

Table 4. Advantages and Disadvantages of Mutual Funds vs. Individual Securities

	MUTUAL FUND ADVANTAGES	MUTUAL FUND DISADVANTAGES
Initial Commission Costs	No-load funds may be less costly to purchase than small stock positions. However, a fund with 12b-1 expenses recovers selling costs over time.	Funds may charge a load fee (usually about 3%) on purchases and a supplemental fee if shares are sold within a short time period.
Total Commission Costs	Funds may pay lower commissions to buy securities than individuals.	Funds may have higher portfolio turnover and hence pay higher total commissions.
Expenses	Passive investors may benefit from the active management provided by a fund in exchange for annual management fees and operating expenses.	Funds charge ongoing management fees ranging between 0.3% and 2.5% annually.
Reinvestment	Dividends and capital gains, even when small, can be reinvested in the portfolio.	Reinvestment does not contribute to diversification.
Security Selection	Portfolio choices made by professionals.	Can't specify specific companies in which to invest.
Diversification	Permits even a small investment to be well diversified within the parameters of a fund's charter.	May limit gains by spreading ownership across many different securities.
Taxes	Certain funds make tax avoidance a goal though some evidence suggests that their returns suffer.	Hard for an individual to tax manage a mutual fund account. New investors may face capital gains taxes on gains earned by the fund prior to their investment.
Adherence to Investment Policy	Keeps investors on track regarding their objectives.	Forces investors to close out one fund and open another to modify investment objectives.

30

identify the 25 companies to place in the portfolio. Mutual funds may offer an attractive alternative to this investor. She might put $5,000 into each of two funds that individually hold investments in 100 companies. By utilizing mutual funds, she effectively spreads her money between more than 100 companies (fewer than 200 because the two funds may overlap their investment decisions) while minimizing her acquisition costs.

Security selection is another critical reason why some investors prefer mutual funds. Many investors lack the expertise to pick companies in which to invest. Past stock picking experiences may have led to disappointment. One selection error that self-investors make is to put funds into last year's winners. Some academic research indicates that plan may be their worst choice. Other investors only buy local company stock because they feel that they know these firms. Maybe they do, but that leaves them vulnerable to regional dislocations. Numerous error possibilities haunt the self-investor. The Chipping system that you will read about below helps self-investors narrow the choice between securities; of course, no system is fool proof. Mutual funds may benefit the self-investor because they employee seasoned investment personnel. However, not all fund managers are equally capable. Worse still, fund mangers sometimes are replaced (investors may not notice), loose their touch, or never really had special expertise (they prospered by following the crowd through a market expansion).

Reinvestment concerns the question of what to do with dividends or capital gains. Our typical investor above with $10,000 of capital had she invested on her own might receive dividends on her stocks at a rate of about 1% per year or $100. That amount is probably too small to justify a new investment in her account. By contrast, most mutual funds would allow her to invest the $100 into more mutual fund shares without a penalty and often without a load. She

31

would then own slightly more shares in the companies the mutual fund was invested in. But most importantly she would have reinvested her funds easily and cheaply.

Finally, it is probably easier with mutual funds to stick with an investment philosophy regardless of whatever perturbation world events or economic circumstances throw in the way. Mutual funds must comply with their charters and maintain the investment posture they advertised. People, on the other hand, may react at the wrong time, to global changes by modifying their investment plan thereby hurting their investment performance.

The remarkable growth during the past thirty years in the mutual fund industry demonstrates persuasively that the pluses in Table 4 overwhelm the minuses. Consider these remarkable facts:

1. From a modest base of $47 billion dollars under management in 1970, the mutual fund industry skyrocketed to $7 trillion dollars by the year 2001 growing by 150 times in just three decades. Inflation adjusting the $47 billion brings the total to only $218 billion in 2002 dollar terms.

2. More than 50% of Americans rely on mutual funds to manage a portion of their wealth[7] with over 36% of aggregate mutual fund balances designated for retirement accounts.

3. Fully 22% of the $15 trillion held in U.S. equity markets in 2000 resided at mutual funds.

With growth in dollars under management has come a proliferation in the number of mutual funds available to consumers; in just ten years (1990 to 2001) the number of stock, bond, and money market mutual funds exploded from 2,900 to 8,300. Accounting for some of this growth is

---

[7] Estimate based on the 227 million mutual fund accounts as of 1999 according to the *2001 Mutual Fund Fact Book*

competition between mutual fund companies[8] but the rest of this growth arises from the creation of new investment vehicles offering innovative services and prospects to investors.[9]

The eight major varieties of mutual fund types are listed in Table 5. Aggregating eight types to just three reveals that equity funds (those buying stocks) hold 49% of total invested funds, followed by money-market mutual funds at 33%, and bond and hybrid bond/stock funds at 18%.[10] Notice the correspondence between mutual fund classifications in Table 5 and our earlier discussion of strategic investment decisions regarding style and type. This correspondence occurs for two reasons. First, funds market themselves to investors who may decide between funds based on these strategic decisions. Second, these decisions underlie the entire investment process.

In the quest for the consumer's dollars, funds label themselves according to investment type and style in line with the strategic decisions investors themselves make. In addition, many mutual funds stress the superiority of their fund manger, i.e., the person (or committee) making the fund's investment choices. Managers are pitted against each other in the battle for the investor's dollars. However, empirical research, for the most part, does not validate the notion that certain fund mangers have more potent skills than do other managers. Generally, the best performing funds in one year revert to being mediocre or even inferior in the next year. Performance reversals result in part from the sectoral specialization of funds (one year's best sectors say oil and natural gas are often the next year's worst

---

[8] The largest 25 mutual fund companies managed 73% of all funds as of December 31, 2000.

[9] See *2002 Mutual Fund Fact Book*, Investment Company Institute, 2002.

[10] Ibid *2002 Mutual Fund Fact Book*, Investment Company Institute, 2002.

sectors) but in part reversal highlights the fickleness of top performance and the manager's lack of miracle attributes[11]. Index funds circumvent the mystic of the manger by investing monies to match the performance of an index such as the NASDAQ 100 or the S&P 500. Index funds compete based on expense charges since their underlying assets are nearly identical.

Mutual fund investors can also make the third strategic decision discussed above, whether to be active or passive, just as self-investors do. An active mutual fund investor occasionally buys and sells funds moving his capital between positions. He may put his capital into money-market funds while he awaits new stock or bond fund opportunities. On the other hand, passive mutual fund investors buy and hold funds for a long time.

The trouble with mutual funds is that most mutual fund investors never consciously make this third strategic decision; implicitly they think that mutual funds are never to be traded or mistakenly believe that the fund manager takes care of that for them. While a few mutual funds are permitted to put the investor's money into a safe short-term sanctuary away from the market at times, the vast majority of funds have charters (rules governing their behavior) that mandate adherence to a rigid investment policy. Most charters require funds to be fully (nearly 100%) invested in a particular market category or sector at all times. In other

---

[11] Managers such as Peter Lynch of Fidelity's Magellan fund, Mario Gabelli and Michael Price, are the exceptions that prove the rule. Most managers fail to achieve multi-year return dominance.

Table 5. Types of Mutual funds

Type	Typical Investment	Variations	Total Return	Risk
Money Market	Short term instruments	May be tax exempt or offer check writing	Very Low	Very Low
Bond	Fixed income securities	May be tax exempt or have different average maturity dates.	Moderately Low	Low
Balanced	Mixes stocks and bonds	May include foreign securities.	Moderate	Moderately Low
Stock Dividend	Common stocks paying dependable dividends.	May be limited to preferred stock.	Moderately Low	Moderately Low
Income	Seek out high income investments	Junk bonds, mortgages, etc.	Moderate	Moderate
Index	Buys an equal weighting of stocks to match an index.	Examples include the S&P 500 index.	Moderate	Moderate
Growth	Stocks	May be aggressive or conservative.	High	Moderately High
Sector	Highly specialized stocks	Very narrow to broad categories.	Moderately High	Very High

words, once they've got your money most funds keep it invested in basically the same way whether or not it is a good idea until you choose to sell the fund. Smart mutual fund investors trade out of funds when they peak (granted it's always a hard call) and buy them back when they are low (also hard to predict). The Chipping philosophy taught below works well with mutual funds as its does with individual stocks or bonds. It guides investors who have chosen to be active in how to move funds into and out of mutual funds in an effort to maximize his investment returns.

IS THE STOCK MARKET THE SAME AS GAMBLING?

This book is about investing. Investing and gambling are opposites like war and peace or love and hate. Arguably some investors became gamblers in the frenetic late 1990s bubble and unquestionably all day traders are gamblers but the distinction between the two types generally exists. Between them sits a third activity, speculating, which has properties of both. Differences between gambling and investing mimic society's progress since prehistoric times. No doubt, the pursuit of a five-ton mastodon by the hunters of a clan of cavemen armed with simple hand-honed spears and rocks was a life or death gamble. But the clan had no way to invest. It had to gamble. Today gambling is not the only way to obtain relief from the biological need to provide for one's family. In other words, for what (providing more for his family) our caveman brethren had to gamble (the hunt) the modern hunter can invest. Gambling and investing are now distinct activities. One can gamble if one wishes just as one can invest if one wants profits. Let's contrast along four dimensions, in Table 6, the three activities, gambling, investing and speculating. Gambling and investing completely diverge in three aspects; in one case, psychic income, they are similar.

Table 6. Comparing Gambling, Speculating and Investing

Activity	Typical Return	Tangible Purchase	Duration	Provides Psychic Income
Gambling	Negative	No	Immediate	Yes
Speculating	Uncertain	No/Yes	Short -less than a year	Yes
Investing	Positive	Yes	Longer often exceeding a year	Yes

All three activities in Table 6 to some degree satisfy the human craving for excitement and adventure. The shrill clanging of slot machines against the backdrop of bright casino lights is aurally equivalent to the steady pulse of stock prices cascading across TV screens and monitors into homes and offices. Beyond this visual similarity there are few other equivalents between a casino and the stock market. In contrast, the differences are many and begin with the expected outcomes or typical returns from each activity. Stock market investors over the past 74 years have earned average returns of 11.3% per annum while bond investors have earned about 5.5% per annum as seen in Table 1. That is, on average, investors have been winners earning money from their activity. In contrast, gambling is a losing proposition. Most gamblers go home with less money than when they started. The odds, as defined by casino rules, are stacked against the gambler in favor of the house and then adding insult to injury the government taxes gambling winnings heavily.

37

Gamblers may rationalize their loses as money spent purchasing enjoyment or excitement. What a remarkable leap the modern gambler has made since the time of the caveman. A Neanderthal hunter who returned home from his gamble empty handed after a long but futile hunt would still need to feed his family; excitement just didn't cut it. Not every gambler makes that excuse. Habitual gamblers, on the other hand, never justify their activities by discussing psychic income (excitement) but instead they convince themselves that eventually their luck will turn.

Stock market investors are woven from a different cloth than gamblers. Also changing the dynamics is the fact that the stock market is not a zero-sum game; you can win without someone else losing. This dynamic creates an enormous psychological divide between gamblers and investors. Gamblers expect to lose while investors expect to win. These expectations are usually met. Consider the equilibrating reaction when they are not. A winning gambler usually decides it's his lucky day and so he returns to the tables and proceeds to lose his winnings and more thereby fulfilling his true expectations. A losing investor on the other hand, tries to change his approach, improve his returns, and thereby fulfill his true expectations.

During intervals of rising stock markets, most participants actually do win at least in the sense of having more money when they stop than when they started. That is, while they may actually have earned a higher return from putting their money into a safe investment like a government bond or a certificate of deposit at the bank instead of into stocks at least their total return has been positive so that their total capital has not been diminished. Few gamblers go home with as much money as they came with. For another thing, society views the two activities differently. Investors who are totally absorbed by it to the extent that they continually work on their strategy and tactics are called wizards or are thought of as being conscientious while those who gamble incessantly are called addicts. The difference is subtle but important. Addiction is bad while diligence in the stock market is good and that's fundamentally because gambling and investing are not the same thing.

Speculators and investors usually purchase or sell physical objects such as a stock (ownership in a company), barrels of oil, or undeveloped land. Gambling on the other hand, the classic zero-sum game, occurs when you and I agree to bet on an outcome devoid of economic activity such as a football game or the roll of two dice. Investing's tangibility yields economic growth and prosperity. That is why governments encourage and support investing and why they view gambling only as an opportunity to generate tax dollars.

Finally, gambling provides instantaneous exhilaration that satisfies the gamblers' need for an immediate fix. Gamblers scratching lottery tickets and hoping to hit a $100 million jackpot or some other chimera are generally less well off than individuals investing their money. In contrast, investing and to some extent speculating, take place over time. No doubt when stocks leap upward investors receive the same endorphin rush as stimulates a gambler but the difference is that stocks rarely jump and when they do there is usually an underlying business or economic reason. Investors are there to make money not to get a fix.

Gamblers and investors love the way their activities pump them up. But investors want more than the fix, they want to be a winner. Excitement and profits are often conflicting goals. Excitement like one feels while watching a horse race or while climbing a mountain derives in part from the element of danger. Seeking profits by investing, on the other hand, entails some level of risk but the investor has greater control over the amount.

This book does not address the psychology of why the drama of speculative markets draws investors who willingly risk their fortune. Although psychology is a powerful component of investing, this book is about winning. It has been written for investors who need a new way to view themselves and a new set of tools that may help them achieve better results.

Chapter 2
The Winner's Circle

My father would tell a story about a man he sat besides at a racetrack. At the end of each race the man would yell out, "I've got the winner!" After getting everyone's attention the man would stick the winning ticket in his neighbors' faces and brag about his horse-picking prowess. After enduring this behavior for six races, my father surreptitiously followed the man to the ticket booth where he overheard him buying a ticket on every horse in the race. With eight horses running that meant he had purchased seven losing tickets and just one winner. Having the wining ticket was more important than making money to him. Maybe winning made him feel like a Thor investor.

Before dismissing this story, reflect for a minute about how in casual conversations, on TV shows or in newspaper articles this character constantly reappears: he is someone who incessantly brags about his unfailing investing ability. The odds are high that this braggart conveniently forgot to mention his investing debacles. I think of my father's story each year when the *Wall Street Journal* runs its annual summary of investing results from the prior year. The table resembles the fictitious one below. The returns reported for each investment class are always surprisingly close though some are positive and others are negative. Usually no category totally dominates. However, at the bottom the table reports a pseudo category that describes the returns that a prescient investor would earn if he daily switched his money between types of investments in order to earn that day's highest returns. This artificial category always overwhelms everything else in the table. An investor who was always right would earn stratospheric returns. However, the data are easily misconstrued. They can be as misleading as what the race track goer who sat besides my father would have reported had he been asked how much profit he had earned that day. No doubt, he would have added up his winners but not included the cost of his losing tickets. Investing is challenging. Everyone has winners and losers.

Table 1 Annual Returns from a Variety of Investment Sectors

Investment	Annual Returns
Equities	+10.5%
Foreign Stocks	+8.2%
Bonds	+7.1%
Gold	-1.5%
Real Estate	+5.9%
Optimal investing: Moving to the Best Investment Each Day	+684.5%

Along similar lines consider the world of hedge fund managers the category of investment advisors reserved for the very rich. As a group they take more risk then most investors and often earn the highest returns. Julian Robertson and the Tiger funds and George Soros and the Quantum Fund are notable though recently retired hedge fund managers. If you think then that hedge fund managers are the best investors, think again. Fewer than 50% of hedge funds reach their one-year anniversary. Many lose most of their capital within months of starting to invest and go out of business.

These tales are not meant to be gratuitously frightening. Rather their purpose is to help readers to realize that investing is neither a game nor a hobby. Yet some people are casual about it. Investing is a highly competitive world. The unprepared and those unarmed with a better system than anyone else are likely to be losers. Following the first three chapters of this book, I present an investing system called Chipping. It has helped me to move out of the category of investing loser and into the winner's circle. It may help you too.

Experienced investors may choose to skip the current chapter and the next and get right into the Chipping material that starts in Chapter 4. I don't blame them and would probably do the same myself if I had just bought this book. However, I strongly urge them to return afterwards to these two chapters so that they better understand essential issues that influence investing success.

DOES HOW YOU INVEST MATTER?

The long-term superiority of equity investments over fixed-income securities on both a nominal and risk-adjusted return basis was established in Chapter 1. Though some investors may not adopt equities as their investment choice because of differences in their time horizons and resources, the remainder of this book is devoted to equities alone. My presumption is that for *Type of Investment*, the first decision posed in Chapter 1, readers favor equities. Given that choice, this chapter concentrates on the *Style of Investing* decision as explained above. It describes the impact on total returns of accepting more risk and shows how various investment styles or systems influence those results. It also discusses how to analyze stocks, how to identify a great company, and how to avoid bad stocks. The final choice discussed above, *Investment Behavior*, concerns the investment holding time period. It is addressed in Chapters 4 - 9 where the relatively short holding period Chipping system is detailed.

Equity selection involves two decisions. With the first the investor decides between types of equities, for example, domestic or foreign stocks or those paying dividends versus those with the potential for rapid growth. Then with the second decision the investor decides which company's stock to buy. This chapter provides insights related to the first question. Chipping is proposed later as a technique for resolving the second equities decision: which stocks to buy.

Multiyear Investment Returns

In an extraordinarily compelling book, *What Works on Wall Street*, James P. O'Shaughnessy reports on a long-term study of nearly every conceivable type of investment style. With data from the past 42 years, he provides average returns and Sharpe Indexes for 66 different types of investments. Serious readers should obtain a copy of his insightful book. Several inextricable conclusions arise from perusing O'Shaughnessy's results:
1. Alternate investment strategies yield vastly different average rates of return,
2. Even small differences in average rates of return generate enormous differences in long-term wealth
3. Investment strategies with higher rates of return do not necessarily have lower Sharpe Indexes.

The first conclusion supports the aggregate data presented in Chapter 1 on differences between returns from equities and fixed income securities though the width of the range between specific investment types is remarkable. O'Shaughnessy found average rates of return over 42 years ranging between 2.62% and 18.62% per year. In other words, an investor who chose the worst strategy over the past four decades earned just 2.62% per annum while the best investor strategy earned a whopping 18.62% per year. Read O'Shaughnessy's book! Some popular investment strategies actually perform surprisingly poorly while other less well-known investment plans do quite well. Knowing the historic success rates of alternate strategies benefits every investor.

The second conclusion derives from the magic of compound interest. A $10,000 investment in the strategy with the highest multi-year rate of return creates a nest egg of approximately $13 million after 42 years. In contrast, the worst yielding strategy compiles a terminal value of not quite $30,000 after the same 42 years[12]. How a 16% annual difference (18.62% vs. 2.62%) leads to a 433 times greater fortune ($13 million vs. $30,000) is explained by the magic of compound interest. Compounding occurs when profits earned in one year are reinvested allowing future profits to be earned on both the original investment fund and all reinvested profits. The advice is simple: find the best yielding strategy, continue to invest in the same way and compounding does the rest.

The third conclusion sounds technical but its meaning is straightforward: some investments provide an inadequate return compared to their riskiness. Excluding three simple strategies, O'Shaughnessy found Sharpe Indexes ranging between 17 and 66. A higher Sharpe Index, as explained in Chapter 1, is better for the investor than a lower index. The scientific interpretation of the Sharpe index is that it describes the number of times by which an investment after adjustment (i.e., after removing the risk-free return and dividing by 100) exceeds its risk level. His data show that some investments provide only 17 times more return than their risk while others provide 66 times as much. Obviously, a higher return for each unit of risk is preferred. Consequently, certain investments studied by O'Shaughnessy dominate their peers. They provide better returns for a fixed amount of risk. What then is the best

---

[12] Other authors such as Suze Orman have written books that describe the role of compounding in investing. In my opinion, nothing describes this impact better then O'Shaughnessy's range of critical ending values from a $10,000 investment.

investment for you? The investor's right choice is the investment category whose average return meets her needs but which has the highest Sharpe Index among comparably yielding investments.

Three strategies studied by O'Shaughnessy are presented in Table 1 to illustrate this paradox. They highlight the importance of Sharpe Indices. Each of the three strategies earned similar average returns. An investor picking between strategies based solely on return would be indifferent between them. Yet the investments differ dramatically in terms of their Sharpe Indexes. The worst of the three investments, the third one in Table 2, has 26.9% more risk for approximately the same return as the best of the three investments. Clearly, the investor must be careful – and use O'Shaughnessy's work as a guide – when choosing between types of investments.

Table 2 Average Returns and Sharpe Indices for Three Investments as reported in William O'Shaughnessy's *What Works on Wall Street*

Type of Investment	Average Rate of Return	Sharpe Index
Type 1	17.10%	66
Type 2	17.10%	54
Type 3	16.84%	52

Shorter Interval Differences

Once at a children's finger-painting party I observed that after enough new colors are added, finger paint turns gray. Applying that logic to investment returns, one might ask whether O'Shaughnessy's data is irrelevant because it spans so many years; that is, has it added so many new colors that its message is ambiguous? The answer to that question is both yes and no. Yes, because patterns of performance across four decades are irrelevant to an active trader who constantly transfers his funds between investments. No, because using return information over any shorter time interval at best establishes potentially unrepeatable patterns and at worst provides information that is misleading and harmful. Certainly though, any buy and hold investor should peruse the O'Shaughnessy data before making an initial purchase.

Short-term traders ignore multi year Sharpe Indices. They seek a return performance similar to the pseudo portfolio described at the bottom of Table 1 that beats all others. While few traders move funds daily, many investors jump between sectors several times a year attempting to catching each at their bottom and selling them out at the top. Some of these traders may adopt the new Chipping stratagem.

Perhaps the best demonstration of how short-term results are misleading is found in a study prepared by The Vanguard Group in which it tracked the top 10 mutual funds in 1991 for the next nine years[13]. These ten funds invested in different types of stocks ranging from multi-cap value stocks (the number 1 fund), multi-cap core stocks (the number 2 fund), specialty diversified stocks (the number 3 fund) and multi-cap growth stocks (funds 4-10). These ten funds were the top performers that year out of 605 funds studied. They were the crème de la crème. How well did they do the next year? In 1992, the top fund of this group came in number 71 out of 687 mutual funds studied by Vanguard; the worst fund, number 8, fell to number 629. Worse still, in the year 2000, the best of the funds, number 10, fell to number 993 out of 4,545 funds studied while the average of the other nine funds ranked 3,442 out of 4,545

---

[13] See "How to Select a Mutual Fund," The Vanguard Group, Web site information obtained May 27, 2002.

funds. Overall the average of the ten funds ranked in the bottom 1/3rd of all funds nine years after their success in 1991. Their performance was abysmal. Woe to the investor who based his mutual fund selection decision on fund rankings for 1991 or any single year for that matter. Just a few years of data are simply too short to gain an adequate impression of future returns possibilities.

PICKING WINNERS: EVALUATING COMPANIES

A key to stock market success is the choice of companies in which to invest. Stories about legendary investment managers ranging from the modern superman Peter Lynch to earlier champions like Bernard Baruch always provide the same take-away message: pick companies destined for success. That advice is fairly useless like saying "if you want to be rich get a job that pays a lot of money." The secret is not avoiding unsuccessful companies any simpleton realizes that. The key is to actually devise a way to select companies that will prosper.

Serious investors have two systems to help pick stocks. They are called fundamental and technical analysis. A third method is to pick stocks by throwing darts at a newspaper and buying companies whose names are closest to the darts. Frivolous investors use this method when they buy stock based on tips from friends, recommendations in newspaper or magazine articles, or whose stock symbols coincide with their own initials. The remaining sections of this chapter explain the basics of fundamental and technical analysis, describe the elusive apotheosis "the great company", and discuss how to avoid buying stock in companies that are dogs.

Fundamental Analysis vs. Technical Analysis

The two primary methods used to evaluate companies are profoundly different. Fundamental analysis involves careful assessment of financial reports, industry and competitive conditions, and related pertinent facts to form an impression of a company's future profitability and share price. Technical analysis studies historical price information to discern patterns of movement. One way to describe the difference between these methods is by comparing how two people that are about to buy homes test them for defects. The first person, the fundamental analyst, looks for holes in the roof, fires up the furnace, and performs similar tasks to verify that everything in it is working. The other person, the technical analyst, studies the home's historic repair record and assumes that past flaws will reoccur. Both analysts may uncover problems with the home. Similarly, both fundamental and technical analysis can uncover stocks whose prices are low relative to what they are worth.

Fundamental Analysis

The fundamental analyst's primary tools are financial statements that companies issue quarterly. The three major reports are the income statement, the balance sheet, and the statement of cash flows. Each contains relevant information. A highly simplified set of financial reports is given in Tables 3a – 3c. The income statement describes how much money a company makes. It's like your year-end W2 statement. The balance sheet describes what the company owns (its assets) and how much it owes (its liabilities). Note that assets equal liabilities; that's why it's called a balance sheet. It contains the same information from a company that a bank asks from you when you request a mortgage or a car loan. The statement of cash flows tells whether the company has more cash at the end of the year than when it started. It's like the school child's marble bag that he counts at the end of the day to tally his wins and loses.

Financial statements provide the inputs that analysts use to create ratios. The reliance on ratios instead of unadjusted raw data occurs because ratios normalize size differences between big multi-billion dollar companies and small enterprises. For example, instead of looking at company sales (obviously sales are larger for big companies than for small ones) to learn about performance, a ratio such as sales per employee might provide better information. Small companies can perform as well as conglomerates with ratios. There are nearly an endless variety of ratios. Each elucidates an important piece of information. For example, comparing net profits ($30,000) and sales ($1,000,000) in Table 3a reveals that Upside Down Inc. has a profit margin (net profit divided by sales) of 3%. Comparing this figure with the margin earned by competitors or with what Upside Down Inc. earned last year helps the analyst to evaluate company performance. From the balance sheet, Table 3b, the analyst might calculate the ratio of debt to total assets ($35,000 divided by $70,000) to learn that 50% of the firm's investment is borrowed. Again this figure is compared with the firm's history and its competitors. Finally, from the statement of cash flows, Table 3c, the analyst might look at cash flow from operations ($40,000) in comparison with total assets ($90,000 taken from the balance sheet) to learn how much cash the company throws off in comparison with its total investment. This is not the place to discuss all the ratios that might be considered. Many good finance/accounting books already do that and interested readers should rely on one of those.

Beyond ratios, fundamental analysis also considers how current legislation, e.g., a new trade agreement, scientific or technical breakthroughs, or any change in the corporate environment might influence a company's future performance. The analyst's objective is to find undervalued companies to buy and overvalued companies to sell. They look for companies that in their opinion have been inefficiently priced by the market. An efficiently priced security is one that takes into account all information about the firm, its products, and its industry. A fuller discussion of market efficiency is provided in Chapter 5. For now though, consider how hard if not impossible it would be for the average person holding down a regular job to out analyze a stock in comparison with a large staff of fundamental analysts employed by institutional investors and securities firms who research them full time. For most investors, fundamental analysis alone is probably not the route to investing success.

Technical analysis

Technical analysis begins with the reasonable assumption that all security prices are determined by supply and demand. Fundamental analysts believe this too. Where the two differ is how the supply and demand for stocks are determined. Technical analysis' other premises are more controversial; that prices move in trends (e.g., rising stocks keep rising) and that stock price patterns tend to repeat themselves. Technical analysts rely on charts drawn from prior price movements to buy/sell stocks. For example, a technical analyst might buy (sell) a stock because it hit a historic low (high) price level or because it "did not break through a price resistance or support level." Additional technical factors examined include trading volume and moving average price levels. Technical analysts look for recognizable patterns in trading data for which their argot includes phrases like a "head and should pattern" or "bear trap." Some people see a similarity between technical analysis and tealeaf reading because when a pattern reveals

Table 3a Income Statement for Upside Down Inc.
(Year End December 2004)

Sales	$1,000,000
Cost of Goods Sold*	900,000
Operating Profit	100,000
Interest	50,000
Taxes	20,000
Net Profit	30,000

Includes depreciation of $10,000.

Table 3b Balance Sheet for Upside Down Inc.
(Year End December 2004)

ASSETS		LIABILITIES & OWNERS' EQUITY	
Cash	$10,000	Bank Debt	$5,000
Inventory	13,000	Taxes Payable	1,000
Current Assets	23,000	Current Liabilities	6,000
Machines	67,000	Mortgage	40,000
		Shareholder Equity (SE)	44,000
Total Assets	$90,000	Total Liab. & SE	$90,000

Table 3c Statement of Cash Flows for Upside Down Inc.
(Year End December 2004)

Cash Flow from Operations	
Net Income	$30,000
Depreciation	10,000
Total	40,000
Cash Flow from Investing	
Machine Purchase	(15,000)
Cash Flow from Financing	
Bank Loan	3,000
Change in Cash	28,000

a reason to buy to one person another person sees a reason to sell. For most investors, technical analysis alone is probably not the path to investing success.

Technical analysts argue that fundamental analysis is flawed because it relies on accounting data that may be manipulated or inaccurate. Moreover, they point out that fundamental analysis in some regards is like searching for a needle in a haystack. Unless you know where to look you won't find anything. Returning the criticism, fundamental analysts argue that past movements in securities prices have no bearing on future profits and hence corporate values and thus should have little to do with current or future prices.

The divide between fundamental and technical analysts is less than it appears since many of them actually rely to some degree on both techniques. Chipping also depends to some extent on both types of analysis. Chippers assume that as a result of the work performed by millions of fundamental analysts and investors that the market is generally efficient (not accurate). Consequently, most securities are reasonably priced, based on fundamental analysis, most of the time. But sometimes something happens to individual stocks that cause their prices to become inefficient. Technical analysis, the study of prior price movements helps decide when a stock price has moved sufficiently to become temporarily inefficient and hence an appropriate target for Chippers.

What Makes a Great Company

The idea of great and not so great companies is central to the theory of Chipping. Chippers only want to buy the stock of great companies. The key question is how do you know when a company is great and when it is not so great. What comes to my mind regarding this conundrum are the immortal words of Supreme Court Justice Potter Stewart when he was asked to define obscenity. He said, "I know it when I see it." To some extent, the same is true with great companies: you'll know them when you see them. Of course, fundamental and technical analysis techniques provide a systematic framework to aid this inquiry. Because Chipping requires relatively quick decision making, I focus my evaluation of company greatness along four dimensions that evaluate its management, operating income and sales, appearance, and solvency. Lets refer to these as the MOSAS test a name derived from the components first initials. These are discussed in turn below.

Sometimes it is not possible to get adequate information along all four aspects of the MOSAS spectrum. Great company decisions can be made on less than four inputs though additional caution should be used. More conservative chippers might refrain from buying a company for which any MOSAS information is unavailable. The MOSAS process works along lines similar to the "black-ball" voting system that clubs and fraternities use to select their members. That is, don't invest in a company that scores negatively along any of the four parts. A single flawed category is enough to create doubts that a company is great.

Management

Of the various attributes required for a company to succeed, excellent management is unquestionably one of the key ingredients. Sure a solid business plan and sufficient financing are necessary too, but without leadership, the other attributes cannot blossom. They will whither like a rose bush planted in the desert. The problem for the investor is knowing how to detect top managers without the aid of in-person interviews or a crystal ball. Just because a firm has been doing well does not mean that its managers are capable. The firm may be prospering despite bad management. Similarly, some failing firms have talented managers who should <u>not</u> be labeled as inadequate just because the company lacks a necessary ingredient, other than management, necessary for success. A problem that often arises when trying to assess management ability is the temptation to rely on fallacious indicators of talent such as school attended, age and previous employment. These indicators each seem to convey solid information. But they don't! There are many examples of good managers who never went to business school or who are young and never worked for a well-known great company.

For these reasons, the evaluation of management's abilities is easier to conduct from a negative perspective (i.e., looking for indications of malfeasance or ineptitude) rather than from a positive standpoint. Most of what is heard or seen in public documents or broadcasts about companies and their CEOs is mindless propaganda and should be ignored. Watch for stains and blemishes that companies don't want the investor to see. Avoid companies whose leaders are in the news because of excessive compensation packages, whose jealously drives away key employees, or who are unwilling to abandon unsuccessful ideas. Likewise, CEOs who blame others for their mistakes or who flit from job-to-job are suspect. Worst of all are executives who accept mediocre performance from employees or in the company's financial results. Corporate travails are common. What is intolerable is when they are not speedily dealt with in an intelligent fashion.

A positive sign of a company moving toward good management is when an executive joins the firm after having succeeded at another <u>similar</u> company. Examples include Paul Pressler who became CEO and president of Gap Inc. following a stint as the Chairman of Walt Disney Company's global theme park and resorts division, Stephen Wolfe who joined US Airlines after working at Republic and Tiger Airlines, and Jeffrey Katzenberg who joined DreamWorks SKG. Of course, prior success is no guarantee of future results as exemplified by Gary Wendt's inability to turn around Providian Financial Corp. after he left GE.

Operating Income and Sales

Corporate income is traditionally measured in several ways. Most common are net income and operating income. Be highly suspicious of a company that reports some other "pro forma" income measure. It is possible that in doing so they have eliminated certain relevant costs from their calculation. Between the two established profit measures, each is more appropriate in different situations. Net income subtracts all costs incurred from sales. In contrast, operating income does not remove interest and tax expense. Certainly

56

net income is a more complete picture of a company's profitability. Yet there are times when operating income, the ability to cover all non-financial costs, is a superior measure because the company is in a developmental phase during which net profits are unexpected.

Great companies report many years with strong earnings growth. The fact that they slipup and miss their growth target in one or two quarters does not make a non-great company. In fact, how a company reacts to adversity, minor though it may be, is also a sign of greatness. However, know why income slipped. If a charge is taken to write off a failed idea and as a result income dips that may not be bad. In contrast, if sales growth slowed while expenses continued to increase that is most certainly bad. Companies that have no operating income are unable to pay production costs. It is hard to imagine how a company without operating income could be great.

No magical profitability hurdle rate exists to differentiate between companies that are great and those that are not. In some cases, a seemingly low profit is acceptable while in others it is a sign of trouble. The arbitrariness is no different than how people change their impressions about food quality before and after a big meal. For example, whether the economy is expanding or contracting impacts how corporations are viewed. Corporate earnings growth of 7% might be weak during a boom period but more than reasonable during slack times. Similarly there are different profit expectations for firms depending on the stage of maturity that their industry is in. Companies just beginning to ascend the growth curve have lower profitability targets while for those reaching their plateau there is a higher earnings target.

Appearance

Great companies have identifiable well-established products/services that are known by most consumers in its marketplace. I call this appearance. One sign of consumer familiarity with a company is when it achieves brandedness. Brand status and appearance are nearly synonymous. The difference lies in non-consumer products/services like natural gas pumping equipment where a company's reputation creates an appearance rather than advertising and promotion, which consumer products companies use to create a brand. Branded companies have appearance but those with appearance do not necessarily have a brand. Branded companies and those with appearance charge higher prices and earn greater profits. That is why Chipping investors seek out companies with appearance.

Of course, not every identifiable branded company survives or achieves great-company status. Everyone knew Pets.com and its offensive sock puppet yet the company faltered and faded away. Coca-Cola and Starbucks, by contrast, are known worldwide and have been enduring great companies. Appearance is the least worthwhile of the four MOSAS signs since it is ephemeral, difficult to compare between companies, and not forward looking, yet it is hard to resist a pretty face.

Solvency

Solvency is the last element in the MOSAS test for company greatness though it is certainly not the least important. In fact, it is probably more important than the other three components combined. If there are any questions about a company's solvency then it is certainly not a great company. Solvency means that the company has an ability to pay its bills and financial obligations in a timely manner. Great companies never fear a sand clock nearing expiration above their head. When such a clock exists, managers are diverted away from the business of business and spend their time searching for new money. Assessing corporate solvency is a fairly straightforward exercise and one in which fewer disagreements arise between viewers than for other MOSAS factors.

The first things to examine in testing solvency are a company's reserves of cash and near-cash items such as marketable securities. They provide a measure of its ability to pay its bills. Note that other assets such as equipment or land are ignored since they are not easily converted into cash. Against this combined cash holdings amount compare the indebtedness owed by the company within a year by combining bank debt and the current portion of long-term debt. A company lacking cash money to pay off its near term indebtedness is not a great company. In fact, some investors want a company's cash to exceed its short-term debts several times over.

Cash shortfalls destroy more companies than anything else. Bloomingdale's ran out of cash before its bankruptcy so to did Enron and TransWorld Airlines (TWA). While it is true that more complex strategic or operational issues cause cash crises, the investor is rarely able to perceive those inner secrets. What is most obvious to the investor and the company's creditors is its cash position. Keep your eyes on the cash. This is a critical source of corporate trouble that can be monitored and avoided.

Identifying Dogs Before Its Too Late

A Chipper's worst mistake is too erroneously put a terrible company onto her buy list. When this happens, the Chipper buys an initial position in the company after the stock conforms with the other Chipping rules that are laid out below. Then the nightmare begins when the not great company continues to decline in price and the Chipper buys more shares, as Chippers do, which puts her deeper and deeper into a hole. This misjudgment is committed on occasion by nearly all types of investors, not just Chippers. But it is worse when done by a Chipper because a) she buys more shares as the stock price falls and b) it makes her doubt her ability to pick out great companies.

The mistake of buying additional stock in a dog is more likely to happen during a bear market than during a rally. When stocks are rising and banks are extending credit, dogs are harder to spot since they hide behind new loans and phony announcements. But dog stocks exist during rallies too. During market declines, dogs come out of the woodwork. During slack times it is necessary to be especially vigilant when evaluating great company candidates. The advice of course is to avoid the dogs and only buy stock in stars. While that is easier said than done, there are certain things to watch out for that may alleviate some of the risk of buying a dog.

The Dogcatcher's 13 Nets

No screen to detect dogs can possibly reveal every flawed company. Applying the list below of 13 items to watch out for when searching for hidden-dog companies may help uncover many troubled firms. Companies that are possibly dogs have:

On their balance sheet
1. Little or no cash.
2. Large amount of debts coming due within a year.
3. Substantial total debts.
4. Soaring inventories and/or accounts receivable.

Dividing balance sheet items by the number of shares outstanding converts them into per share amounts. For example, a company with $10,000,000 of total debt and 5,000,000 total shares has $2.00 of debt per share. Yahoo Finance already performs this calculation for the cash item and several others. Comparing balance sheet concepts per share against a company's per share stock price gives the investor a basis to recognize values that are too high or too low. For example, a company that has $4.50 per share of cash, zero debt per share, and sells for $4.50 per share is quite possibly a great company. The investor appears to get the business for free after buying the cash. Though deals that seem to good to be true often are, sometimes they are real. Likewise, it is doubtful that a company with $0.05 per share in cash, $9.75 per share of debt and a stock price of $15.00 is a great company.

On their income statement
5. Falling sales.
6. Disproportionately more workers hired than the change in sales.
7. Falling income but a paternalistic attitude toward employees.
8. Results so much better than every company in its industry that it's highly doubtful that the company is doing this well.

Declining sales cause concern. Some companies are more facile at building themselves up to accommodate growing sales than they are reducing their infrastructure when sales fall. Bloated companies have reduced or negative profits and cash flow and may face a cash crisis. These worries are somewhat reduced for companies in cyclical industries when the economy is in a recessionary phase. Don't forget that high technology is cyclical too and that the acceleration (deceleration) in sales and profits on the upswing (downswing) may outpace what other industries experience.

Worker salaries are responsible for the majority of costs in most industries. Look out for companies that over expand their work forces, give overly generous wage settlements, or who express a reluctance to lay off superfluous workers. These may indicate the possibility of a future crisis.

Finally, be especially careful of a company that according to its income statement is doing very well in fact far better than any other company in its industry. While it may be that the accounts are true, there is the other possibility that the accounts are fraudulent. My former student Henry Garelick provided this observation along with a list of offending companies. I call it the phenomenon of the "rat wearing a tuxedo." This observation is tempered if the company is rapidly gaining market share or has achieved a production cost advantage that puts it beyond the reach of its competitors.

<u>As part of their demeanor</u>
9. Controlling stockholder is dishonest and self-dealing.
10. Suspicious or hard to understand accounting practices.
11. Self-dealing among the board of directors.
12. The accounting firm or the company's directors or officers resign.

Self-dealing and dishonest officers and directors are a sure way to get burnt by a stock. Shocking tales abound of companies whose assets were pilfered by persons with the responsibility for protecting them. It is very hard to uncover nefarious plots from afar. For that reason, the only defense is to rely on my grandmother who said "fool me once shame on you, fool me twice shame on me." <u>Never</u> buy a stock whose executives or directors were found guilty of corporate fraud or subterfuge or who though never indicted or convicted are "known" by everyone to be crooks. Such infamous characters run many companies. On the other hand, Chipping opportunities exist when over zealous prosecutors or newspaper journalists falsely accuse a company's officers or directors.

Several things to watch for that may help uncover self-dealing and dishonesty are

- Excessive pay to executives. Yahoo Finance Profiles report executive compensation from both salaries and stock options.
- Children, spouses, or parents are also officers or directors of the company.
- Excessive stock option awards.
- An Internet search turns up prior allegations of misconduct.

Flimsy accounting is also hard to uncover by outsiders especially those who aren't accountants. Yet sometimes the accounts just don't make sense to anyone. For example, before treating it as a great company a firm with negative operating income and positive net income should be examined more closely. Similarly, there may be good reasons for a company to change its accounting firm, but the fact that it occurs at all should be cause for suspicion.

In the Stock Market
13. Stock prices that have gradually fallen while competitor's stock prices have risen or stayed constant.

Despite my reluctance to rely on the stock market for signs that a company is great, sometimes things are learned by comparing the stock performance of one company against its peers. Yahoo Finance again provides an easy framework for this comparison. After requesting a stock quote for one company simply click "Competitors" beneath the quote for a list of other firms in the industry and then click on "Chart" to simultaneously graph the price of two or more companies. A company whose stock price lags its major competitors for no discernable reason such as an announcement about slow sales may have fundamental issues that have not yet been revealed. On the other hand, the company may be getting set up for you to Chip it.

If a safety check list of 13 items seems excessive, recall the damage that a dog company inflicts on a Chipper. Obviously, it is worthwhile expending major effort to try and avoid disaster. The 13 watch points are organized not according to importance but rather by where the investor can find out about them. The sections labeled as coming from company income statements, balance sheets, and stock market price history are readily accessed in Yahoo Finance's "Profile" section, a URL below each Yahoo stock quote. Investigative skills help to uncover items listed in the "company demeanor" section.

Don't limit your research to the dogcatcher's list of 13. Each company is unique and may have its own peculiarities that appear on its balance sheet, income statement, or elsewhere. Also, no list can discover a well-conceived and hidden fraud perpetrated by high-level company executives so keep your funds diversified.

CONCLUSION

Making money on the stock market is rewarding and fun. It's not necessarily easy. Avoiding bad companies and picking good ones may help you to be a stock market winner. Before trying your hand at Chipping, understand the principles discussed in this chapter and keep them in mind as you trade. It is especially important to frequently review the MOSAS concepts about what makes a great company and the dogcatcher's 13 nets for detecting stocks to avoid.

Chapter 3
Lessons from an Irrational Bubble

Congratulations! You've just survived the implosion of an irrational stock market. Of course, this wasn't the first time the stock market has experienced a debacle. Throughout history markets have regularly reached outlandish levels. Sometimes prices go up too much, other times they decline too far[14]. The simplest explanation of stock price movements is the twin emotions of fear and greed. Fear leads to sales by investors worried about getting wiped out. Greed provokes purchases by investors who think they know how to get rich. Usually fear and greed are only tenuously related to reality. Stock sales (fear) and purchases (greed) driven by emotions lack basic sensibility. When fear seizes markets they move strongly to the downside sending stock prices to unjustifiably low levels[15]. Likewise, greed creates a buyer's frenzy that pushes stock prices to absurdly high levels. Market emotions are normally in check because the number of anxious investors roughly balances out with those who are greedy. But sometimes the pendulum swings too far and nearly everyone believes that bad times are coming (fear) or that there's easy money to be made (greed). Market irrationality occurs when investor sentiment becomes extreme and commonly shared among investors.

O.K., emotions cause mispricing. But does that mean that at other times in the eyes of all investors stocks are priced correctly? Apparently not because every investor who sells thinking the price is too high is matched by an

---

[14] The classic book on this topic is *A Random Walk Down Wall Street,* Seventh Edition, by Burton Gordon Malkiel, (W.W. Norton & Company), 2000.

[15] The book to read about this is Philip A. Fisher's, *Common Stocks and Uncommon Profits and Other Writings,* (Wiley Investment Classic), 1996.

investor who buys because she thinks the price is too low. Yet the idea of a fair price based on sound principles is not unreasonable. While a right price for stocks may not exist, well-established company-valuation methodologies provide a good starting point for estimating a possible range of reasonable market prices. We will return to company valuation issues later in this chapter.

The recent stock bubble germinated in January 1991 with the NASDAQ market resting at a level of 355 and flowered continuously until the end of the 1st quarter of 2000 when that market peaked at 5,120. Over 9-¼ years of mania, an investor who stayed invested in the NASDAQ composite earned 33.2 % compounded per year. This astronomical return was totally out-of-step with history when over a 74-year span the average larger company equity earned 11.3 % annually. During the euphoria, starry-eyed analysts argued that a "New Economy," unlike prior markets, permitted stock prices to travel in one direction while corporate earnings went in the opposite direction. Everyday different start-up companies with few sales and no earnings received billion-dollar market valuations while profitable old-line companies were valued far lower. Whenever anyone questioned the arithmetic they were told that the market had outgrown its old rules and patterns. How right the worriers were!

The Internet craze was propelled by the exciting idea that in the future there would be new ways to conduct business, communications, and information gathering. One kooky-eyed idea after another came to market including shopping on the web for products ranging from heavy furniture to inexpensive cosmetics or the home delivery of videotapes and prepared foods within an hour. Investors envisioned themselves getting in early and making huge profits. Greed overwhelmed intelligence. Otherwise rational individuals used hard earned money to buy dream stocks in untested and unprofitable businesses. Their choice of companies in which to invest was influenced by the fact that a stock had been $50 a share last week and was now $65 a share. The bubble mania accelerated when some lucky investors sold the $65 stock a month later for $100 a share. They used the proceeds to buy other stocks and then convinced their friends and neighbors to do the same. Dreams of riches and luxury clouded everyone's eyes.

Did the average investor miss any clues that foretold the eventual collapse of the bubble? The answer is a provisional yes: provisional because the forest concealed many of the trees. An unsophisticated but interesting clue was noted in a previous stock bubble (1923-1929) from Bernard Baruch, a stock market guru, who gained fame when he sidestepped the great depression. Baruch remarked that he knew the market was too high when his shoeshine boy began to give him stock tips. Similar signs surfaced in the 1990s when investment clubs, taxi drivers and high-fashion models became noted investment experts[16]. In the late stages of the market correction of 2002, this type of ill-informed sage extolled the opposite prediction that the market would never recover and that all hope was lost. Their squawks sounded like Chicken Little who worried about the sky falling.

Another clue to the frothy stock market came from a conventional yardstick. It says that on average equities should return to the investor an amount equal to the nominal change in GDP plus any dividends received. The rationale behind this theory is that the aggregate stock market cannot out pace the economy for too long. To appreciate this sentiment consider how odd it would be if the economy were permanently stagnant but the stock market was increasing by 10% per year. The situation is unfeasible because who would pay more for assets whose

---

[16] See *The Beardstown Ladies' Common-Sense Investment Guide: How We Beat the Stock Market-And How You Can Too*, (Hyperion), January 1995.

earning's power were flat. During the 9-¼ year frenzy on Wall Street the compound annual growth rate in nominal GDP was 5.8%. With dividends kicking in an extra 1.2% or so the overall market according to this benchmark should have grown about 7.0% annually. With the technology sector outpacing the growth rate in overall spending by at least 5%, NASDAQ stocks according to this yardstick would be expected to have grown about 12% per year, not 33% per year. The additional compounded growth in the NASDAQ of 19% per year was not supported by economic activity but by speculator's hopes and dreams.

In September 2002 when the bubble finally burst and the dust settled (my guess), the NASDAQ market fell to a level of about 1150. At that point, the return earned by an investment in the NASDAQ from January 1991 through June 2002 was about 11%. Although calculations like the one above that posit a "natural" rate of increase in NASDAQ stocks of about 12% have no magical predictive power, it is interesting that the market decline stopped when prices had fallen to a level supportable by economic activity, profits, and cash flow.

A final overlooked clue that the stock market had risen too rapidly was the reckless market for initial public offerings (IPOs). IPOs enable private companies to sell some shares to the public and thereby raise needed capital. Early stage companies with limited operating experience and financial results initiate most IPOs[17]. The lack of history makes it difficult for investors to implement traditional corporate valuation models that require estimates of future performance. For that and other reasons,

---

[17] The other use of IPOs is when large companies spin off divisions or when large family owned companies issue shares to diversify family holdings. The largest IPO was conducted by AT&T when it spun off AT&T Wireless, it cellular division in April of 2000 raising $10.62 billion. United Parcel Service went public in November 1999 raising $4.38 billion.

IPOs have historically lagged the overall market. Academic research reveals that the average IPO from 1975 – 1984, prior to the market bubble, returned to investors about half of what investors in existing companies earned[18]. Returns were substantially greater during the bubble. During 1999 for example, when more than 400 companies conducted IPOs, the average IPO stock rose by 200% by the end of the year[19]. Not only did this return exceed the historic IPO return by nearly 20 times but also the sheer number of IPOs was more than four times the usual rate[20].

The epitome of IPO craziness was the December 10, 1999 offering by VA Linux Systems Inc. (LNUX) at an offering price of $30 per share. LNUX's product is software that conceivably could replace Microsoft's Windows operating system. That dream pushed the price of the stock on opening day to a high of $320. The stock's closing price on day one of $239.25 gave it a record first-day return of nearly 700%[21]. By 2002 LNUX's price had fallen to less than $1.00 per share. With over $55 million in the bank, no debt, and a shrinking loss the company might actually survive and prosper. But purchasers of the security on opening day probably had no chance to ever earn a profit.

Most investors were caught flat-footed by the market decline and lost a great deal of money. Part of the responsibility for this rests on their reliance on the buy-and-hold philosophy that remains popular among investors, and part rests on their having missed the obvious signs of an

[18] See Jay Ritter, "The Long-Run Performance of Initial Public Offerings," *Journal of Finance*, Vol. 46, No. 1 (March 1991), pp. 3-27
[19] See Ilana Polyak, "Funds That Lived by the IPO in '99 Are Dying by Them This Year" *TheStreet.com*, 5/17/00 5:38 PM ET.
[20] For example, there were only 110 IPOs in 2001. See "Venture-Backed IPOs Remain Scarce in Q1, But Valuations Stabilize" National Venture Capital Association, April 4, 2002.
[21] See, Jack McCarthy, "VA Linux Soars Almost 700%," IDG News Service, NetworkWorldFusion, December 10, 1999.

overheated market. These investors should not pity themselves but should learn from their mistakes. They may need a new stock trading system and may need to become more vigilant. Remember this anonymous saying, *"Fools repeat their mistakes, the wise make them only once."*

WHY DO STOCK PRICES CHANGE?

Why do investors buy stocks? The answer obviously is to make a profit. But how do investors make money when they buy stocks? The answer again is straightforward: by selling it to someone else at a higher price. The danger with this repartee is that it sounds like a Ponzi scheme that works until the last investor discovers that he has no one to sell out to[22]. Others have argued that the portion of the stock market bubble related to Internet companies was actually nothing more than a giant Ponzi scheme. But what about the value of stocks in the broad market including wonderful companies like Procter & Gamble Company and The Coca-Cola Company? There must be more to stock valuation for companies like those than just being able to sell out to someone else at a higher price.

A Basic Model of Corporate Valuation

A question I always ask students is whether they would be willing to buy shares in a highly profitable company that has decided to never pay dividends, buy back any shares from holders, or sell out to another company. They usually answer yes and defend their answers by saying something like, "Well Microsoft has never paid a dividend."

---

[22] See, *The Rise of Mr. Ponzi* by Charles Ponzi, Inkwell Publishing, November 2001.

Unfortunately for students, the answer is that a company that does not have a mechanism to provide the investor with cash, at some point in the future, has no value. That does not mean that a company must pay a dividend or buy back stocks for it to be valuable. Many companies grow and reinvest all their cash flows and then later sell out to an acquirer. Investors receive their share of the proceeds after the repayment of debts. Other well-established companies pay out a substantial portion of their cash flows to investors as dividends. Still other companies regularly repurchase some of their existing stock causing the price of remaining shares to increase. In order for a corporation to have any value, at some point in the future there must be a flow of money from the corporation to the investor.

Stocks are valuable because of their potential to eventually provide the investor with money. If there were no doubt about the number of dollars a company would give its investors or the date when those funds would be dispensed, there would be no uncertainty about how much its stock was worth other than personal differences in discount rates to account for the time value of money. But in fact, there is enormous uncertainty about the size of corporate cash flows both this year and in all future years. Companies pronounce and analysts prognosticate but in the final analysis each is doing nothing more than making an educated guess. Vagueness about corporate cash flows emanates from uncertainties about future economic conditions, geopolitical considerations, and a host of corporate concerns including whether new competitors will emerge and how consumers will react to new products.

From uncertainty, a consensus of opinion gradually forms and the investing community reaches an "understanding" of what the future is likely to hold for a firm. The consensus incorporates expectations about the firm's future cash flows, the riskiness of that expectation, and a sense of how the firm will allocate cash flows between dividend payments and reinvestment. Not everyone agrees with the price level based on that consensus. Conflicting opinions lead to selling by investors who think that the price is too high and buying activities by those who believe that the price is too low. New information can abruptly shift the consensus view and result in substantial changes in market price. Disagreements produce investors with a contrarian view who sell into a buying frenzy or who buy when others are selling.

Where Do Dream Stocks Come From?

Children on a playground sometimes get hurt when they climb too high on a gym apparatus. Part of the fault lies in their over developed sense of confidence which they adopt after successfully reaching the next highest rung. To some extent, dream stocks that everyone "has to own" follow a similar pattern with successively higher price rungs being reached until eventually reality overtakes dreams and the stock tumbles back to earth. Whenever a dream stock's price tumbles my thoughts turn to the story of "The Emperor's New Clothes." After the little boy revealed the fact that the emperor was naked everyone else saw that too. Similarly, when $100 dream stocks tumble down to $1 a share or go bankrupt everyone who lost money in them understands why their prices collapsed. But it's too late at that point. A better strategy would be to develop a trading discipline that avoids dream stocks entirely. The typical investor has no capability to evaluate the truthfulness of claims associated with dream companies or to uncover possible accounting frauds that may undermine their price.

The pattern of overpricing in dream stocks follows a path like that depicted below.

1. An entrepreneur emerges with a good business idea.

2. A public company is created.
3. Ambitious sales and earnings targets are articulated.
4. Targets are reached or exceeded for several years.
5. Naïve analysts forecast continued prosperity by extrapolating prior gains.
6. Competition between analysts creates excessive optimism.

In rare cases, an unstoppable company continuously beats the numbers. An adolescent Microsoft comes to mind. A more likely outcome is that investor soon gets caught holding the bag on a mediocre company that has been priced like it was a diamond. This problem did not arise along with the Internet. It has always haunted investors. For example, decades ago when Bausch & Lomb Inc. popularized contact lens its stock price got too high. A prominent business magazine belittled the market's valuation of the company's stock saying that its price only made sense if every man, woman, child, and dog in America eventually bought a pair of contact lens. The stock price plummeted once the truth was revealed; in the same way that the Emperor ran away once his nakedness was discovered.

Investors with limited expertise or knowledge are probably advised to avoid dream stocks completely. That of course means that they will never own shares in the next Microsoft. While that is regrettable, it also means that they will avoid owning stocks like Pets.com, VA Linux Systems Inc., and Global Crossing Ltd. The number of dreadful companies far exceeds the number of prospective Microsofts. Dream stocks are like hot potatoes: woe to the one left holding their shares when the truth is revealed.

Differentiating between Value and Hype

The prior chapter discussed ways to uncover great companies and differentiate them from their opposites: the dogs. Here the concern is to differentiate between great companies and those that are merely hyped. This new task is more difficult because hyped companies are pruned to look like great ones; they work in exciting fields, their sales are explosive, and there is a steady stream of "planted" newspaper and magazine articles describing their greatness. Those responsible for promoting a company's shares – investment bankers, brokers, and company executives – always paint the rosiest picture possible. Sometimes they exaggerate and overstate a company's true potential. The question then is "how can a normal investor avoid the merely hyped companies and find the truly great ones?"

The task is not easy. When annual reports of both types of companies are compared they look about the same. Both are glossy with pictures of fancy gadgets, upstanding looking executives, fancy buildings, and words of hope and promise. Hype is sneaky. I think there are two fundamental ways to separate wheat from the chaff. The first and most important is to focus on cash flow. Great companies generate a lot of cash. In the final analysis, hyped stocks rarely provide a steady flow of cash back to the corporate coffers. Though they always provide a reasonable sounding explanation for the lack of cash: for example, sales are growing rapidly requiring reinvestment in our business or we are too early in the corporate development stage. Maybe what they are saying is true and maybe it's accurate. But it may also be that they are growing rapidly because they are giving their product away and as a result they don't earn a profit. Stick with companies with healthy cash flow.

The second bell weather for me are companies whose products I personally use and adore. Gillette is a great company because I rely on its blades. Wendy's makes a dandy salad and so it's a great company too. And I love getting lost in a Barnes and Nobles store which is another great company. Ask your kids or grandchildren what is hot among their generations and then check it out for yourself. The same applies to reviews in legitimate media outlets. Of course, a good product may be supplanted when an even better one comes along.

Avoiding hyped stocks is probably as important as learning to find great companies. Error on the harsh side to avoid losses. Begin by thinking that a company is only hype and then gradually move it into the great company category when it passes muster on a number of tests. Keep the testing period short, otherwise great companies priced right, see the upcoming Chipping chapters, will get away.

Prior Experience Leads Us to Chipping: A New Way to Invest

Joseph Kennedy the father of our 35th president was a very rich and powerful man. When asked how he had achieved this wealth he is purported to have replied, "I always sold too soon.[23]" The buy-and-hold crowd must have gasped for breath when he uttered that phrase. Their mantra, in contrast, is to buy stock in companies and then never sell out. Kennedy's maxim is similar to the expression "the bulls (optimists) and bears (pessimist) both make money on Wall Street, it's the pigs that lose." The point is that until profits are banked they remain at risk.

Consider just a few of the disastrous companies we've talked about so far in this book. WorldCom began its trading life at $8 a share in 1993, rose to $64 in 1999, and in 2002 fell to $0.07. Enron Corp was a sleepy stock

---

[23] Others ascribe this quote to John D. Rockerfeller, Baron Rothschild, and Bernard Baruch. I am unsure of its true origin.

trading below $10 a share from 1970 – 1992; it remained a sleepy less than $20 stock until 1998 but then exploded up to $90 a share in 2000. In 2002 it is trading for about $0.10. Precipitous dives pummel not only disaster bound companies but strong mainstream companies as well. During the first six-months of 2002 when markets were swooning and the Dow Jones Industrials average fell by approximately 10%, the slide in some of the Dow's components was much steeper[24]. For example, General Electric Company fell by 40%, Hewlett Packard Company by 42%, AT&T Corporation by 44%, and even venerable IBM by 36%. These companies suffered declines that were four times greater than the fall in the Dow Jones Industrials as a whole. Buy-and-hold and suffer the consequences. As my friend and colleague Don Margotta says, "I've never seen a stock chart that goes in only one direction." The stock price of all companies go up, down, and sideward. You are not safe owning shares into perpetuity in any company not even IBM, General Motors or even Microsoft. All of them had sharp declines in their stock prices during this period.

Will Rogers the famous cowboy humorist who died in 1935 used to say that making money on the market was easy, "Just buy stocks and sell them when they go up, and if they don't go up don't buy them." His unachievable prescription for profits means never buy a stock that is going to fall. Obviously no system except for not investing at all can avoid all instances of falling stock prices. But Rogers did get half of the story right, when stocks go up sell them and make a profit. The question remains though which stocks should be bought?

The remainder of this book details the Chipping system of investing. Chipping is not a guarantee of stock market profits nor is it a system that will work for everyone. Read

---

[24] The decline in the NASDAQ was nearly 35%.

Part Two
Approaches to Chipping

Chapter 4
Chipping Towards Stock Market Success

IS CHIPPING FOR YOU?

Two types of people play the stock market: winners and losers. Who are the winners? Everybody makes money on a stock once in a while, but that doesn't make him into a winner. Winners are persons who make a profit most of the time they invest and who, at the end of the year, have a big profit to show for their efforts. By big profits I mean 20% or more on your investments. 20% is not an outrageous goal; wealthy individuals investing with hedge funds expect returns at this level or higher. Losers may make money too sometimes, but overall they would benefit from putting their funds into a bank certificate of deposit or by letting a mutual fund manage it. Losers far outnumber winners. I would guess roughly that losers comprise at least 75% or more of stock market participants.

The first step in becoming a winner is to understand what differentiates winners from loser. Winners generally adhere to well-established systems for beating Wall Street. By a system I don't mean a superstitious ritual such as only buying stocks that start with the letter "T" or selling investments 15 days after they are purchased. A system is a set of rules that define good investments from bad investments. Examples of systems are buying stocks with low price-to-sales ratios or sell after losing 10% of the original price. A number of systems exist; if you find one that works for you then by all means stick with it. Losers generally follow no system but instead behave like Tweedle-Dee and Tweedle-Dum, constantly changing direction, trying to follow the leader, and always being a month or a fad behind. If you don't have a system for investing then don't invest. Highly sophisticated players, using state-of-the-art computer analysis tools, populate the stock market. You can't beat them by throwing darts at a board.

This book introduces a new system for profiting from the stock market. I call it Chipping. I call the system Chipping because one tries to earn many small profits just as a golfer hitting a chip shot doesn't try to hit the ball very far. A hole-in-one because when investing whether you put the ball into the hole in one shot or ten so long as you earn a lot of money that's all that counts.

Chipping your investments is like chipping on the golf course: golfers say that it's the short game (meaning when you are close to the hole) that determines the final outcome. Stock market chippers put quick week or two week of 10% or more into their pockets and do that over and over again. Obviously, chipping is not the only system and it may not be the right one for you. In fact, if you are currently making money on the stock market, or generally do make money there, that is you are a winner, then this system may not be the right one for you. Stick with what is working but save Chipping for when your system fails you. This book aims to help the majority of stock market investors, the losers. Some of them may have the personality, inclination, time and finances necessary to become a successful Stock Market Chipper™. Hunters as described in Chapter 1 are perfect candidates for Chipping. They are willing to take a chance both on something new and on an investment system that at first may seem counterintuitive.

About five years ago and for many years before that "I was a stock market loser." That's my confessional statement, which is similar to what someone says at an Alcoholics Anonymous meeting. For me, that simple statement summarizes about 25 years and thousands of dollars of stock market experience. Understand that I didn't lose money every year. But more often than not my income tax return was devoid of any net stock market gains. Even worse, on the front page of the Federal 1040 Tax Form there generally appeared the mark of the ultimate stock-market loser: a $3,000 write off of investment losses, the maximum allowed even when my actual losses were greater. Gradually I realized what I was doing wrong: I was listening to the wisdom of Wall Street gurus. What I failed to understand was that they and the investment houses they worked for were more interested in making money for themselves than in making it for me. Their mantras change very little over the years and so I'm sure that you have heard them too. So frequently are they quoted that many investors think of them as "stock market gospel." Messages like *hold your winners*, *sell your losers*, *don't trade too often*, and *let your winners mature into long-term capital gains*. If you've listened to these mantras and made money, then by all means keep doing so. But if like me these rules set you up to be a sheep among Wall Street wolves then admit that their system does not work for you and consider becoming a Stock Market Chipper.

Whatever your age, gender, socioeconomic rank or family status making a profit on your investments ought to be your goal. If you're not profiting from your current system then find one that does work. Don't be lazy or ashamed. If you are currently a loser make the loser's confessional I professed above: "I am a stock-market loser," and then get on with the task of finding a new way to invest.

WHO CAN BE A GOOD CHIPPER?

Almost anyone can be a good chipper. All that it takes is the ability to recognize when a great company is a good value, and the courage and financial strength to act. Probably the easiest way for me to initially explain Chipping is by describing the way that I grocery shop instead of how I invest in stocks. Each week at the grocery store I purchase a week's supply of items for my family. Having performed this task almost religiously for the last 30 years I have assembled a fairly sizeable and reasonably accurate mental database of grocery store prices and pricing tactics. This gives me a good sense of how much things are "worth." In addition to pricing information, when I enter the store I also know the quantity of each good at home in storage, the amount of dairy, meat, vegetable and fruit that my family consumes weekly, and how much money I have available to spend. I am also aware of which goods can be kept in storage for future consumption and which must be consumed within the week. So what do I do then? Goods like milk or bread which spoil quickly I buy each week. But nonperishable or freezable goods like canned soup or meat, I buy extra quantities of when they are priced low on sale and hold them in storage for future consumption. In other words, I know what things are worth and I act on that knowledge in order to minimize my grocery bill. For example, suppose I know that the store where I shop usually sells chicken breasts for $1.69 per pound but this week the price is just $0.99 per pound. Moreover, suppose that I believe that the price next week will return to $1.69 per pound or even higher. What is the logical thing to do? If you usually buy one pound of chicken breast each week, why not buy five pounds this week, store four pounds in the freezer for consumption over the next month, and hope that the store has another chicken breast sale before you run out of frozen breasts. That way, you pay $0.99 per pound for chicken breasts that you and the store feel are worth $1.69.

Hopefully, you buy your groceries the way that I do. If you don't you're wasting money and as importantly you may not be psychologically attuned to being a Chipper. A

Chipper is a person who takes advantage of opportunity, whether it be saving $0.70 per pound on chicken breasts or making a quick $200 on a $1,000 investment. If you do not care about saving $0.70 per pound on chicken then I doubt that you will be able to buy the type of stocks that are good Chipping candidates and then hopefully take quick 10% or 20% returns on these opportunistic investments that are the hallmark of Chipping.

WHY DO YOU INVEST?

People invest for many different reasons; some to diversify their assets, others to create a college education fund or a retirement pool, still others to earn a living. Each of these goals is compatible with Chipping. Chipping is a strategy that may help achieve many financial targets. Chippers invest for one reason: to make money. It is their sole objective. If that is not your investment motive, then Chipping may not be the stock market strategy for you. A Chipper aims to profit from virtually every trade she makes and gladly takes her profit as quickly as possible even it comes in just an hour, a day, or a week. Notice I'm not an advocate of day trading. But on the other hand, if you earn a good profit in several hours time take it, since it may be gone tomorrow. Generally I expect that you will have to wait several weeks or months to achieve your profit target.

But let's return to Chipping. How well can a Chipper do? Obviously, the answer to that question depends on what happens in the overall market. A rising stock market pulls up most stocks while a plunging market, as in July 2002, pushes everything down even great companies. Some Chippers are better than others at picking great companies. Evaluating a Chipper's performance may be obfuscated by her holdings of shares that are priced below what she paid for them: since she purchases temporarily out of favor stocks; a falling market exacerbates the syndrome. During bull markets her inventory contains fewer issues in negative territory. Secondly, Chipping's results depend on the investor's ability to only buy great company shares that have fallen substantially in price. Chippers hold large cash stockpiles. This helps them avoid the larger losses that fully invested investors experience during weak market periods but reduces their gains during rising markets.

Let's use me as an example. In 1999, I made 300 stock trades on which I took a profit 285 times. I had a 95% success rate. I was a winner. Yes, I ended the year holding other issues that were in the red but I also had a large cash position. OK you say, but that was a good stock market year so what happened in 2000 when the market was weaker. In 2000, I traded 1,000 times and earned a profit 950 times about the same success rate as the year before. Again I was a winner. My inventory of unrealized losses was larger than in the year before. 2001 was also miserable for the overall market. I traded nearly 400 times in 2001 and reported profits on 84% of those trades. Unrealized losses in inventory grew too though my cash position remained high. Earning small amounts of money most of the time you invest can lead to outstanding investment returns. Money held as cash remains invested in money-market funds. Most of my capital is always held as cash waiting for an opportunity to invest. Capital held as cash money is not at risk and so it becomes a safe part of your investment holdings. Obviously, I do not promise or guarantee similar returns to anyone. But then, this book is not about you giving your money to me. Its purpose is simply to teach you another way to invest better.

What Does Making Money Mean?

Certainly everybody knows what it means to make money. These days from an early age most kids say that they want to grow up to earn a million dollars. Whether that is a healthy attitude or not is not the topic here, but the question highlights how you must think differently when you invest as a Chipper. Chippers don't think in terms of the number of dollars earned on an investment. They take the professional's approach of calculating returns in percentage terms. Suppose you invest a $1,000 in a stock and then sell it a week later for $1,100. Yes it is true that you only earned $100. The professional investor would calculate your returns in percentage terms instead and say that you earned 10% on your invested funds. Then since there are 52 weeks in a year she would go on to say that on an annual basis you earned 520%. If your investment were held for two weeks, you earned 260% on an annual basis since there are 26 two-week periods in a year. If percentages confuse you don't get hung up just keep Chipping away and making money.

Donald Margotta a colleague at Northeastern University who taught me a great deal about the Chipping investment system tells a joke about a multi-millionaire who was giving a talk at a famous business school. Afterwards a precocious young student asked him how he had gotten so rich. In response he said, "I buy them for $10 and sell them for $15 and make my 5% profit." The point of the joke of course is that the man made a 50% profit and not a 5% profit and that he wasn't school-smart enough to know that but yet he had developed a profitable business system where his product sold at a 50% mark up.

Chippers are investors who take their profits off-the-table and put them safely away. No, Chipping is not like Day-Trading. This is a very important point. Day-trading is an investment strategy in which the investor puts a lot of money into one stock that has been rising and then hopes that it goes up by a small amount, say 6 cents. After the stock rises, the theory says to sell out and reinvest in another stock. The stratagem has consistently worked well for few people. I don't recommend it. Chipping takes a totally different approach than Day-trading. A Chipper makes small investments that are held until a reasonable profit is earned. The definition of reasonable, the size of investments to make, and which stocks to buy are major subjects of this book.

The question posed above about "What Does Making Money Mean?" has both a simple and a complex answer. The simple answer is that making money means not losing any. The complex answer is that you should earn enough money to compensate you for the risk of pulling your money out of the money market and putting it into the stock market. Both answers guide the Chipper. A Chipper knows that it is better to get out of a stock that turns against you with a $1.00 profit then to hold on to it while you incur a paper loss of $150.00. However, the Chipper's goal is not to make $1.00 on a stock; the goal is to buy great stocks that let you earn returns of 10% or more in as little as a month so that your annual rate of return across all investments exceeds 20%.

Who Are You Investing for Anyway?

If you become a Chipper, don't be surprised if friends, stockbrokers, and business associates laugh at you. They may even start calling you funny names. Just ignore them and hopefully count your profits. If you are more interested in being a conformist then you should probably not learn the Chipper Way™. This book is for people who are interested in learning a new system that may guide them to making and keeping a profit on Wall Street. Think about this: If those people, your so-called friends, actually knew what you did all day to make a living, they would probably laugh at you for that too. How you invest is nobody's business but your own and the government's and Chipping may make both of you happy: you because your profits and total income may go up, the government because your tax payments may rise.

People who aren't laughing at you may be smirking instead. These know-it-alls are people who have heard and subscribed to the latest wisdom from the wizards of Wall Street. The truth is they don't know anything more than you do. As a Ph.D. economist, I am constantly amazed listening to TV pundits talking about fairly complicated economic phenomena - such as what the Federal Reserve will do next week or how foreign currencies may react to US interest rates changes - as if they actually knew something about the topic. But then months go by and I hear the same authorities giving a totally opposite explanation for the same phenomena. The reason is that talking media heads must always say something – imagine our shock if they said, "gee we don't know why that happened." Anyone who smirks because you advocate trying the idea of Chipping is probably mystified because the current top sages of Wall Street didn't tell her about Chipping and therefore "you must be ignorant." Ignore them; see if the method helps you make money. If it does stay with it, if it does not, then listen to your friends.

WHO ARE YOUR HEROES?

Everyone has a hero. Young ballplayers want to be Roger Clemens, aspiring politicians emulate Bill Clinton or George W. Bush, and students of the stock market talk about Berkshire Hathaway's Warren Buffett, the vulture investor Marty Whitman, or the immortal Benjamin Graham and David L. Dodd the original value investors. These renowned stock market gurus are legendary for turning relatively small investments into extraordinary sums of money. Unfortunately, if you want to be a Chipper they cannot be your idol. Chippers do not pursue fame and should not aspire to becoming fabulously wealthy. Fame brings its own problems and the ambition to become wealthy breeds a reluctance to sell winners and leads investors back to the old way of buying and holding stocks. You'll need a new set of heroes if you want to be a Chipper. A great Chipper is someone who trades often, holds stock for short time periods (get in and out), and who earns above average rates of return on his invested capital. The only similarity to hope for between a great Chipper and one of those celebrated investors is that they both earn a lot of money.

Chippers should focus on making money by investing and not on hero worship. Too many people idolize larger-than-life individuals (such as Warren Buffett) who have found a system that works well for him but which cannot be emulated by ordinary individuals. I don't think Chipping suffers from that same fault though I readily admit, and you may agree, after you have learned the system, that it requires more work and diligence than what many investors currently put into their "business".

A QUICK OVERVIEW OF CHIPPING

Before presenting the Chipping technique in greater detail in the forthcoming chapters, lets overview the method at this early stage so that you better understand what is to come in the succeeding pages. It is succinctly described below. As with any summary, hold off on your

89

questions at this stage since the synopsis is designed to be short and sweet.

A. Only buy stock in great companies. There are so many outstanding companies that there is no need for you to take a chance on a firm that might be great someday or which was great some time ago.

B. Only buy great company stock after its price is hammered by a major news announcement (such as missing its earning's target by 1 cent) that the market interprets extremely negatively (cutting the market price by as much as 25%) but which in fact is not really that appalling.

C. Only buy small amounts of that stock. The temptation to overload on a specific issue because the company is so great and its price appears so low is overwhelming at times yet it must be controlled. You are not a wizard who knows the future. Keep your purchases small in case you buy too soon or the company turns out not to be so great (never forget Enron).

D. If the price goes down more, then buy more shares but never put too much money into one single investment.

E. If the price rises by a reasonable amount, sell the stock. Avoid the romance of thinking that the price will recover all of its recent losses and then some. Get your profits out and wait for the next Chip.

Chapter 5
How to Chip

A SHORT COURSE IN CHIPPING

After reading the preceding chapter you may want to get ready to Chip on Wall Street. What do you do next? To begin with, if you don't already have one, open a brokerage account. That step is free. Stick with well-known Internet brokers like Ameritrade (currently charges $10.99 per trade), Brown & Co. (currently charges $5 per trade), or E-Trade (currently charges $14.99 per trade), for two reasons: 1) they offer substantially lower commissions than traditional brokerage houses that can save you up to 90% or more, and 2) Chippers are unwilling to pay extra for and unlike ordinary investors don't need broker dispensed information on which stocks to buy and sell. Pick your broker based on commission schedules (how costs change as more shares are purchased), extra fees they charge for using limit orders and for real-time quotes, the rate of interest they pay on uninvested cash (very important if you follow the recommendation to hold a sizeable cash position), and additional services provided such as level II quotes which reveal how many buyers and sellers are standing in line just out of view of the best bid and ask price. Don't buy more services than you need. Most stock research is already old (its affect is already in the market price) by the time the small investor gets it so don't pay for it. You might consider opening an account with freetrade.com (a subsidiary of Ameritrade) or brokerageAmerica.com both of which currently offer commission-free trading. Determine if they will pay interest on uninvested balances and if they don't you might use one of these as a secondary trading only account. Then follow the five-step Chipping system described on the next few pages.

First, put as much free cash as you can spare into the brokerage account. Most of this money should remain as cash in a money-market fund most of the time. You probably need at least $5,000 in the account initially in order to hold a sufficient number of different stock positions at one time. Since Chipping will be a new system for you, be sure that the $5,000 is money that you can afford to lose without changing your lifestyle or shirking financial responsibilities. Remember, at this point, we don't know whether you have what it takes to be a Chipper.

Second, restrain yourself so that you don't rush to buy stocks. Think of the child discussed in Chapter 1 who visits a candy store. After a quick sugar rush he returns home exhausted and empty handed. Staying with the analogy, you want to visit the candy store but only to get the feel for the place, to learn what prices are charged, and to stake out types of candy that you would buy if the price were right. Sitting with your capital invested in a money market account earning interest won't hurt you. Patience is the number one virtue of all investors but especially so the Chipper who must learn to wait for opportunities. Yes, it is true that sometimes you wait too long (in the candy store analogue, all the candy of one type sells out) and you fail to buy a stock that rises but there are thousands of other stocks that you can buy. Never rush to buy because you are afraid that the price might rise: let it. You should only buy stocks that you are completely comfortable owning because they are great companies and because their price is right.

Third, once you decide to buy a stock, begin with a small position. Using a $5,000 account as an example, you might buy an initial $750 position in a stock that you think is a good Chipping opportunity. The reasons for taking small bits are simple: 1) you don't know when a falling stock price reaches its bottom, and 2) you don't want to over invest in any one company. After you buy a stock the odds are about 50:50 that its price will rise or fall. If the price goes down by 5% or 10% more and you still like the company buy more: perhaps $800 more if you gain confidence that it is nearing its bottom or $600 if you think the bottom may still be a little bit lower. If the price goes up after your first purchase, do not buy any more. Never chase a stock back up! Let it go and turn your attention to other issues until it is time to sell.

Fourth, if the price rises quickly and substantially after your initial purchase because you did pick the bottom, then sell the stock. The goal is to earn a good return in a short period of time. For example, earning 10% net of commissions after a week is fabulous; 5% in two weeks is still great; 10% in 2 months is wonderful. The point is that by selling out you actually pocket the profit. Too many investors ride the "loser's roller coaster": they buy stocks, watch them go up, grow greedy and envision the stock doubling or tripling, watch them fall, and then finally sell out at a loss. That is not the Chipping Way™. The Chipper seeks to take a sizeable profit as soon as possible. Of course, if you only have a 1-2% profit after 3 weeks and you feel that the stock or the market is about to fall then sells it. Here too the 50:50 odds statement applies. That is, after you sell the stock about half of the time it will keep going up. If it does, ignore that and do not let it affect your psychology. Keep telling yourself that you made a profit and that you'll buy the stock back again someday when and if its price again becomes advantageous.

As time passes you will have bought, sold and then possibly re-bought a fairly large number of stocks. Spreadsheets such as Excel or Lotus 123 can help you to keep track of prices paid, prices received, and profits earned. Take a few minutes at the end of each day to update the spreadsheet; never fall too far behind or you will miss some wonderful buying and selling opportunities. You will also want to keep track of current market prices. Tracking lots of stocks, some owned, some previously owned, and some that you might own someday, is not as difficult a task as it sounds. Yahoo Finance is a fabulous way (more on this in Appendix B) to track issues, their current stock prices, current news, and to graph their stock price movements. Other free web services are also excellent. For example, to keep track of companies that I recently sold but might someday want to repurchase, I maintain a Yahoo portfolio entitled, "Stocks to Buy Back Someday." Generally, I don't watch these stocks during the day but review their prices only occasionally. My experience has been that the vast majority of stocks that rise after I sell them come down again and usually, within a month or two, are priced lower then where I sold them at. The 50% or so of stocks that fall after you sell them become immediate candidates for future repurchase especially when their prices decline substantially. Keep track of these issues in another Yahoo portfolio labeled something like "Watch These Stocks Closely."

Using care in selling and buying stocks can greatly increase your return so try to watch them during the day and learn where they trade. Chipping is not about finding the next Microsoft. If you know how to do that then you definitely don't need to Chip. In other words, when a stock recovers a good percentage of its recent price drop sell it. Don't be a hero and watch the stock go up and then back down again. There's nothing wrong with selling it today and then buying it back again someday when its price falls again. If its price doesn't fall again forget it and find another stock to buy. Never fall in love with a stock. If you profit from a stock and it falls in price again, maybe you can make more money on it by buying it back again. But only buy back stocks that continue to meet the definition of being a great company and that are priced advantageously. If its price keeps rising after you sell it, forget about it.

Fifth, and finally, try to avoid stocks that can hurt you. I don't expect you to only buy winners. That's not possible. What the system expects you to do is to buy stocks whose prices have already been badly hurt by public announcements, ratings or recommendation changes, or other corporate events so that you only risk market-wide changes by holding or buying more shares. One approach to finding great companies is to consider what products you or your employer buys in a manner similar to Fidelity's Peter Lynch's recommendation to buy companies whose products you know. With thousands of stocks available there is no reason for you to buy an unknown company whose stock price is shattered by an announcement. There are too many great companies that experience similar disasters and whose future existence you can almost take for granted. Of course, that advice didn't work on WorldCom, but frauds are the bane of all investors.

A RESTATEMENT OF THE SIMPLE RULES

To invest in the Chipper Way™ follow the five brief points listed below when buying and selling stocks. Obviously, that alone will not guarantee that you make a profit but it may provide you with a system with clearer investing targets than the ones you currently use.

- Only buy stock in great companies.
- Wait to buy one until its price is dramatically reduced by a not so bad announcement.
- Buy a relatively small amount of stock at first.
- If the price goes down more buy.
- If the price rises quickly, by about 10% or so, sell the stock.

That's it, that's all it takes to be a Chipper. But like so much else in life, the devil is in the details. The rest of this book is devoted to helping you with the details so that when you begin to Chip you will execute the plan well.

How and when these five points are implemented makes the difference between success and failure. The devil is in the details so pay attention. The problem as a Chipper, or any investor for that matter, are a number of critical decision points regarding which stocks to buy and when to sell. And yet the investor is armed with incomplete information. What you'd really like to know is when a stock is going to go up and by how much. That is never going to happen. The way out of this conundrum is by following one of two approaches. Some investors conduct their own research or do so jointly with fellow investors. Others rely on Wall Street firms to advise them. Regarding the first approach, self-study, I don't think that it is realistic to believe that you can out-research Wall Street. My former student Henry Garelick is the exception to the rule. I've actually seen him discover financial errors in documents companies have filed with the Securities and Exchange Commission (SEC). For the rest of us, research can only bring us so far. Concerning the later approach, relying on Wall Street, unless you are a big investor Wall Street advice will arrive "a day late and a dollar short." The Chipper Way™ provides another solution to this problem. It offers a system that requires less research but more patience and strict adherence to a plan.

Lets start with first principles: what is the value of Wall Street research? The academic finance literature argues that the stock market is basically efficient, meaning that most of the time most stocks are predictably priced. Notice, I did not say accurately priced, instead stock prices are predictable meaning they reflect what is know by the public. The three variations to the efficiency argument each provide a refinement to the definition as seen in Table 1. The weak form argues that the market is cognizant of systematic price movements such as the stock of an ice cream seller falling during the winter and rising during the summer. According to the weak-efficiency theory, investor expectations of price increases and decreases will by itself smooth out cyclicality in prices. The semi-strong form of the argument contends that there is no information available in public sources such as magazines, newspapers, or SEC financial filings that will enable an investor to buy stocks and beat the market. The theory argues that the market has already factored that information into prices. The theory's strong form goes the final step and says that prices reflect all information including inside data that is unavailable to the public. If true, traditional Wall Street advice has little value.

Table 1 Forms of Market Efficiency

Variation	Meaning
Weak	Stock market prices reflect all the information contained in past price movements.
Semi-Strong	Stock market prices reflect all public information.
Strong	Stock market prices reflect information.

Which variation is correct is the subject of intense academic debate in finance journals and at professional conferences. My personal opinion is that for fairly large public companies that have a number of analysts following them, the weak form is undoubtedly true, the semi-strong form is probably accurate, and the strong form may be correct. I have less confidence in the theory for small companies or those that are ignored by analysts. Along these lines, evidence of a "small-firm effect" in which a portfolio of small-company stock outperforms the overall market in limited time frames is fairly persuasive. Efficient prices probably exist most of the time for companies that have sales in the billions of dollars, are followed by numerous investment firms and hundreds of analysts, and are household names or sell well-known products/services.

The intuition behind the efficiency argument, in part, is that when many investors study a company and trade its stock, opportunities are removed to beat the market by trading that company's stock. All such discussions are risk adjusted. That is, a highly volatile company's stock might rise by more than the overall market but that is consistent with its of its greater risk of going up or down. People believing the efficiency theory may put their money into index funds that mimic the entire market or portions of it.

The counter argument to efficiency starts with a nursery rhyme: "all the kings horses and all the kings men couldn't put Humpty Dumpty back together again." The notion expressed in this childishness is similar to Robert Schiller's argument in the book *Irrational Exuberance* that in fact not many people independently research a company; what they all do is simply chase earlier investors. That is, if investors follow momentum and if analysts copy each other then they are all chasing a set of stocks that are rising. Consequently, stock prices may not be efficient after all. It should be noted that several months before Enron's collapse only one out of dozens of analyst believed anything was wrong. However you come out in the efficiency argument, you may still find the intellectual motivation to Chip to be compelling.

The discussion above about the small-firm effect is an example of an anomaly from market efficiency. Other anomalies exist too. The small company anomaly arises because the majority of Wall Street analysts consciously omit many small firms from scrutiny. They argue that their time is better spent focusing on large companies like Wal-Mart or GE.

The opportunity to Chip arises, in my opinion, because of another anomaly from market efficiency. The argument proceeds as follows:

1. Most of the time large company stocks are probably correctly priced at least according to the dictates of semi-strong market efficiency.
2. Market psychology is extraordinarily powerful and can disrupt efficiency. If you doubt this, review the irrational level to which stock prices rose during the NASDAQ boom. Prices were not efficient then either. Stock prices rise and fall by too much when circumstances activate powerful psychological levers.
3. The release of bad company news can push stocks prices down by too much. At that moment their prices are less than efficient and thus anomalous.

This anomaly creates the opportunity that I call Chipping. But Chipping requires more than just buying the stock of a great company that is unfairly punished by bad news. A Chipper must also develop the determination to take profits rather than to hold on hoping for even bigger profits. A Chipper is an investor who tries to find a great company whose stock price has declined by "more than it should have" as a consequence of a negative report, news release, court finding, executive departure, or any other influential circumstance and who sells out and takes her profits after the price partially recovers. For most investors, the hardest part of the equation is selling out and taking profits when the price partially recovers from its fall. Chapter 8 reveals the stages of Nirvana that Chippers work to achieve. Learning to sell winners is one of those stages.

Criticism of Chipping may come from Wall Street acolytes reluctant to believe that there is anything new under the sun. They may contend that Chipping is just another name for the well-known phenomenon of a "dead-

99

cat bounce" which Wall Street uses to explain how the stock price of dying companies can rise on a good day. If so, these critics misunderstand Chipping's entire premise. Chippers buy stock in great companies not those going out of business. Moreover, the cataclysmic downward adjustment in the stock price of a great company is not expected to continue for more than a day or two. In contrast, dead-cat stocks are on a one-way trip to oblivion.

A few brief thoughts on what constitutes a great company are appropriate at this point. Obviously, not every company whose stock price falls after a news report is a great company. The investor must somehow separate the wheat from the chaff otherwise their portfolio will consist of a bunch of dogs whose stock prices are tumbling. Further confounding the selection task is the unavoidable fact that intelligent people will disagree about the definition of a great company. No matter how the question is phrased – "is this a great company" - each investor hears the words differently. Some focus on the company's performance last year, others consider how it is currently doing, and still others try to assess its future. A company which was great last year but which has no future is decidedly not a great company. The proper perspective is forward-looking, but how far ahead? Certainly, today's health is relevant since financial exegeses can derail the best-laid plans, yet future results are the key. Great companies will be around in the future, will be larger and more profitable in the future, and have the human, financial, and technical resources necessary to get to the future.

A tactic that will help aim you in the right direction is to avoid asking the direct question – is this a great company – and instead ask a series of defined questions such as:

- Will this company's products continue to dominate the market place?
- Does this company have sufficient cash to get to the future?

100

- Are this company's debts too large, scheduled to be repaid too soon, or requiring interest payments that exceed its ability to pay?

But even these straightforward questions may yield tangled results for a number of reasons. To begin with, the future is beyond everyone's vision. Your guesses are just that: guesses. Second, not even company executives have fully integrated how the firm's plans may interact with actions by current and future competitors. Third, the overall stock market depends on the sentiments and convictions of countless entities and individuals each of whom acts in his own perceived best interest. For these reasons, you may reap more benefits from focusing your questions narrowly on the company and its products:

- Did you buy their product and if so why or why not?"
- Is their management first-rate? or
- Have they introduced a steady stream of new and innovative products?

The second set of questions allows the great company decision to be based more on personal judgment. Of course, that only helps if you know the company and buy or use its products.

A friend of mine Richard Omohundro once taught me an important lesson about financial prices. He said, "A speculator is an investor who buys a bond at par." Par is a financial term for original or issuing price, which for bonds is usually $1,000. What Dick meant is that when the investor pays full price for a new bond, he is taking a great deal of risk because something harming its credit worthiness could reduce the value of the bond. In contrast, buying the bond of a great company after bad news is announced and its price falls to $700 is less risky because the market has already heard the surprise. This is one of the truest statements you will ever hear even though it conflicts with what Wall Street asks you to believe. Paying $100 per share for stock in a great company contains a similar risk; if the shoe falls, the price is vulnerable. Buying the same stock at $60 after a not so bad announcement is less risky.

When is a stock price hurt badly? A central tenet of Chipping is to only buy great stocks after their prices tumble following a corporate announcement. But when have they tumbled enough? If a $100 stock falls to $80 there's no doubt that its been hurt, but if its price falls to $60 next week, it wasn't really hurt that badly at $80. You will need to exercise personal judgment here as to when the price is near its bottom. There is little that I can tell you other than that on the day companies report their bad news, two things generally happen. First, they trade enormous volumes of stock maybe five or 10 times their normal daily quantity. Second, the price plunges almost instantly; in the example above, the stock might open at $81, trade down to $77, and then close at $80. Whether the price will rise or fall on the day after the news is out and thereafter is the Chipper's big question. One of the hardest Chipping decisions is when to buy. I usually wait until the next day following an announcement or at least until the market is about to close on the first day. Chapter 6 discusses how real-time quotes help after you make a commitment to buy.

Sometimes your damage assessments about when to buy will be right and other times they will be wrong. Hopefully you can bat a little better than .500 so that you are right more often than you are wrong. The Chipper does not need to hit the exact bottom; that would require skills only Houdini possessed. The task is to not pay more than is necessary but to get in while the stock is priced inefficiently. Always be patient in your buy decision because if there's one thing that we know for certain it's that stocks go up and down. They never just go straight up. An old trader's truism that "stock prices always go up more than they should and decline by more than they should" is generally true and explains some of the reason that stocks go down (they went up too much) and why they go up (they went down too much). That's why stock prices keep changing: they are searching for an elusive equilibrium which itself is constantly moving. Prices go up and down too much because the underlying motivation behind many stock purchases (greed) and stock sales (fear) are irrational psychological impulses often independent of reality. But it is these overreactions that create opportunities for Chippers. So be sure to let the psychological impacts work themselves out of the market before making your purchase.

Stock prices face two types of risk: one that is market specific and one that is company specific. The finance literature uses erudite expression for these but company risk and market risk tell the whole story. Company risk is specific and includes things like the possibility that the CEO dies or that a valuable patent is declared invalid. Stock prices move quite dramatically when battered by a company risk factor. Instantaneous price declines of up to 90% occur after surprise negative company announcements. Market risk results from geopolitical events and macroeconomic conditions such as changes in interest rates, tax policies, or governmental expenditures. Market timers try to profit from this risk by buying stocks when the overall market is low and selling when the market reaches a peak. Economic forecasts are instrumental though imperfect aids to their decision-making.

Company risk affects the stock price of individual firms. Company risks include unexpectedly lower earnings, losing a court proceeding with major financial implications, a competitor announcing a new product line or price reduction, or other news that leads the investment community to revalue the firm. In deciding which stocks to Chip, be careful not to confuse reactions arising from market risk and company risk. Chippers are looking to buy stocks that have lower company risk because they have just released what is hoped to be all of the bad news. Company and market risks always exist. Since "a falling tide lowers all boats," a stock that you Chip may continue to fall in price after making its announcement because the overall market declines. Buying stocks after they have removed most of their company risk leaves you confronting just market risk. In my experience, most Chipping candidates trade fairly independently from the broader market immediately following their sharp price decline. In contrast, buying a stock whose price declines in synch with the entire market leaves the investor facing company risk and further market risk. That is, the stock may continue to fall because either the entire market declines or because this company releases unanticipated bad news of its own. It is truly challenging to pick the top or bottom of the cycle in an individual stock's price. Timing the overall market, is an even tougher challenge. However, in my opinion, it is easier to pick a stock price bottom after the price tumbles following a major news release.

Chippers want to avoid buying companies with too much company risk. This is absolutely essential for the Chipper system to work. Be sure you understand the implication of this instruction: you will never buy stock in the supposedly fantastic company that your neighbor just made a killing on or that a financial magazine is currently touting as the next Microsoft. Those types of companies have enormous company risk. Let somebody else invest in them. A Chipper might someday buy stock in those companies if they truly are great companies and if they reveal some sort of problem or if a brokerage firm downgrades the stock and if their price plunges precipitously. My favorite buy is when a brokerage firm lowers its earnings forecast for a great company from $0.50 cents per share to $0.48 per share, for example, and the stock price plunges by 35%. Yes that actually happens. I don't know why people sell the stock over a $0.02 earnings decrement but they do. I view it as an attractive candidate for Chipping if it passes the great company test. You will need to decide relatively quickly if this is a great company because in not too many hours or days after the stock opens off 35% or so, investors called "bottom fishers" begins to feed on it and the price may rise. But patience is always a virtue and you are always better off letting one get away than buying one that you shouldn't.

Market risk, on the other hand, is the possibility that the whole stock market declines. The decline may affect all stocks equally, or may particularly devastate issues in a particular industry or that are associated with a specific commodity, technology, or region. Markets decline for many reasons including higher interest rate, inflation, loss of investor confidence in corporate financial reports, wars, or slowing job growth to name just a few. Most stocks get caught in the market's draft and rise or fall at the same time as the trend. As the economy approaches a recessionary period, market risk grows and stocks in general begin to fall. Because a Chipper tries not to hold stocks for very long, market risk is reduced but it remains a substantial problem. A dramatic downturn in the overall market can delay and greatly reduce the price recovery of beaten-down great company stocks. In my opinion, though, already-trashed stocks are good candidates to beat a falling market.

If a great company's stock falls $20 to $30 a share as a result of a general market decline, the stock retains its company risk. While its price may rise from that point onward because the entire market recovers, the stock may instead give the investor a nasty surprise caused by the revelation of a company risk factor. In contrast, when the price of a great company's stock falls from $50 to $30 because its legendary CEO is retiring or because it foresees modestly slower growth over the next two quarters, the investor who buys those shares after the announcement faces mostly market risk with little accompanying company risk. For most companies, it is not always clear why a stock price declines. However, in the case of stocks that are Chipping candidates, it is always clear why their price has fallen: they just released terrible (at least in the market's eyes) news. Subsequent to an announcement, company risk still exists but if the company has come clean, what remains may be insignificant.

Consider the steep price declines of high technology companies during 2001 and part of 2002. Network Appliances' stock fell from $57 to $22 per share and then to $5.18; Corning Inc. fell from $52 to $9 and then to $1.10; and Nextel Communications Inc. fell from $26 to $11 and then to $2.50. Were these market or company induced declines? It is not always easy to tell. During the same time period, prices on the overall NASDAQ market fell from 2471 to 1110. It is tempting to argue that since these three companies had steeper price declines than the overall technology market that they must have suffered at least some company shock in addition to the market risks that all companies faced. That statement may be true for some of these companies and they may or may not be good candidates for Chipping. But never buy stocks just because their price has fallen.

It is also critical to realize that individual stock prices move at their own separate pace (called the stock beta) and not in step with the market. Betas are discussed further in Chapter 6. Some stocks go up and down more quickly than the market while other do so more slowly even without releasing shocking company news. The three stocks mentioned above, Network Appliance (166%), Corning Inc. (186%), and Nextel Communications Inc. (400%), for example, each rose more rapidly than the 74% run up in the NASDAQ market during 1999. These firms have high betas (2.60, 2.49, and 1.91 respectively as of October 2002) and thus their price perturbations exceed market averages. Forgetting these companies, the point is that it is impossible with total certainty to find companies that have exhausted their company risk by simply comparing price declines to the overall market during falling market periods. High beta stocks fall more than the market decline on average simply because they have more volatility. To reduce uncertainty about reduced company risk, I advise you to find companies with less risk by watching the today's winners and losers list found in the newspaper or on line. Find companies whose prices are down by 15-30% or more following a news announcement. Then make sure the new really isn't that bad and that they are great companies. These are Chipping candidates.

Another concern with possible Chips is whether "the other shoe" will drop after you buy a stock that has fallen steeply following some negative news. Its never possible to know this for sure though some degree of comfort can be taken when a company reveals several bad-news items at one time. The release of multiple facts may be an indication that better times are coming and that the company is trying to get future negative surprises out of the way now. You might even wonder if executives of the firm are overdoing it. Perhaps they plan to use this opportunity to scoop up some of the depressed shares themselves or to issue stock options that exercise at the low price. Perversely, I am also comforted when on the day of the price decline/announcement major brokerage firms downgrade their assessment of the stock. These may go, for example, from "buy" to "neutral" or "hold" to "sell." I view their wistful change of hearts as an attempt to "close the barn door after the cow has gotten out," but for the Chipper the downgrade announcement generally has positive results: it pushes the price down still further.

A rushed buy or re-purchase decision may result in the acquisition of an $80 stock that has fallen from $100 before all the bad news has come out and it falls to $60. On the other hand, excessive procrastination, similar to a deer being frozen in the glare of an on-coming car's headlights, delays the initial buy or re-purchase decision too long. Keep track of how well you time decisions. Make adjustments such as buying stocks sooner or later depending on your own successes such that you improve your decision-making. Of course, each stock's trajectory and each trading day's activity are unique and as a consequence you should not measure your abilities against absolute precision because that is an unreachable standard. As mentioned above, companies that reveal all the bad news at once are your best buy candidates.

In October 2000, the SEC promulgated Regulation FD (full disclosure), which requires companies to publicly announce "material nonpublic information" as opposed to selectively dispensing it to large investment houses. This action aids the Chipper by putting them on a more equal footing with large investors. Historically, companies revealed news to analysts before disclosing to the public; stock prices would decline and the average investor had no understanding of why. FD is a tremendous improvement for the small investor. Companies that announce an array of bad news items synchronously may be cleaning house of future impediments to price rises. A clue to the presence of this strategy is when companies write off things that you don't understand.

Knowing when to sell a winning stock involves different issues than knowing when to buy a stock whose price is falling. Remember that no seller always picks the highest price at which to get out. Condition yourself to accept the fact that after you make a decision about half of the time the stock price will continue to rise. Chipper's Nirvana is reached after this and other conditionings take place. The key to Chipping is to take profits after achieving your percentage return target. The adage mentioned above about stocks always going up too high applies in the long run, not to today's price. The Chipper wants to buy and sell repeatedly before the long run comes. Over time you will learn whether you are setting targets too high or low and can adjust future targets accordingly.

The homily "don't put all your eggs in one basket" is well known by all. The Chipper's rule of initially buying a small amount of stock draws from this folk wisdom. The essential reason for this rule is that despite your great patience in watching a stock price drop, you are still highly likely to pay too much. People who do that often kick themselves in the shin and say, "I should have waited." That phrase is barred from the Chipping vernacular. No one can consistently pick the bottom. That doesn't mean that you want to overpay when you buy; rather when the price drops further buy more of it provided that the company is and truly remains a great company. Additional stock purchases at lower prices reduce your average cost of ownership and raise your ownership position to a larger number of shares. Keep in mind, that these separate purchases should probably be sold off individually once each has achieved your return target. After you become a strong believer in the Chipping method your vernacular will acquire a phrase that must sound absurd to a nonbeliever but which I have stated many times to myself when a stock price drops after I first buy it: "Great, now I can buy more of it at a bigger discount." What was a good buy to me at $10 per share is an even better buy at $9. Before making a second purchase reflect on whether this company might be another Enron: a stock whose price is on its way to zero. If you have any doubts about it, hold off on your second purchase because it is always better to be safe than sorry. You are more likely to make a second purchase when the stock is a blue chip, well-known company as opposed to a flash-in-the-pan high technology or other high-risk company. On the other hand, Enron was a blue chip company.

Keep tract of each purchase made of the same company's stock as a separate item in your inventory.

Know that some of the stock in that company cost you $12 per share, some $10.50, and some $9. Then sell each group at its own time. That is, should the price recover to $12 sell the $9 stock and maybe the $10.50 stock too. Intermediate sales yield profits, reduce your dollar investment in the firm, and give you capital to buy still more if the stock falls back again due to market or company risk factors.

Another reason for keeping your purchase quantities small is to avoid owning too many shares in any one company. This is especially important if you are worried that one of your beaten-down companies could go bankrupt. National data shows that about 3/4ths of 1% of all companies fail each year. The percentage is substantially lower for listed companies especially those on the New York Stock Exchange (NYSE). That's a good reason to keep your Chips confined to larger companies like those on the NYSE. Assume that your "great company calls" have about the same risk of being dead wrong as the national bankruptcy failure rate in which case you should expect that about 1 out of 100 of your great companies is a dog that will go bankrupt. Owning fewer shares of possible future dogs is an advantage gained by keeping purchase quantities small. If you are worried about the $5 or $8 commission incurred from buying small quantities, then sit down and do the math. Suppose you buy 40 shares of a $30 stock for $1,200. If the price later falls to $27, a 10% decline, and you then buy another 40 shares for $1,080, the extra $8 commission saves you $112 net. Isn't $8 a fair price to pay to save $120?

Buying more on a price dip is a well-known averaging technique known as dollar-cost averaging. Mutual funds push the idea but since they are paid a flat percentage fee based on investment size, they recommend that you dollar-cost average each month whether the price goes up or down. Obviously, a Chipper would never agree to that proposition (more on this later when we discuss Chipping mutual funds). Buying more on a dip serves a secondary Chipping purpose: it increases your stock holdings up to a respectable size since you began with a modest purchase.

At this point, let me describe my personal best Chipping story concerning Genzyme Molecular Oncology (GZMO). Learning about bioengineering from students I decided to watch these companies that might cure cancer someday. GZMO showed up on my screen one day when its price fell substantially to $3 per share within a month of its initial public offering at $15. I bought some. Twice I unloaded the stock at $3.30 and quickly earned a 10% profit. Then the stock got away from me and ran up to $11. Usually I won't repurchase a stock until the price falls below my sale price, $3.30 in this case, but GZMOs prospects really attracted me back. I felt it was a really great company especially given that its parent company is Genzyme Corporation. I bought some when it fell to $9, then more at $8, $7, $6, $5, and finally still more at $4. Not long after that GZMO began to move up when other people decided (probably based on the recommendation of Wall St. analyst) that they had to own biotech. I cannot explain why the market decided at that moment that biotechs were good investments, it just did that's all.

When the market realizes that the great companies that you own are in fact great, the Chipper takes profits. Chippers are expected to sell out early and not look back. I tried that with GZMO but my holdings had grown to a respectable size and people just went crazy wanting to own it at any price. I sold some at $6, them some at $8, more at $12, $18, $25, $35, and finally some at $41. My average cost was about $5.00 per share and my average sale price was about $25.00. Don't aim for returns like that. I just got caught in a stampede owning a great company when everyone else wanted to own it. Did I feel bad when the stock was $41 that I had sold most of my shares earlier at lower prices? Absolutely not! This is a critical psychological state for Chippers to achieve. In Chapter 8 Chipper's Nirvana is discussed. Nirvana is an emotional state of mind that you should aspire to attain. Regarding stock sold at a lower price than its current level, a beginning Chipper is likely to regret earlier sales; when he gains some experience, he regret them but knows that they were the right thing to do; and eventually when he reaches Nirvana he doesn't regret them at all.

I don't regret earlier sales of GZMO stock. I made a profit on each trade, and made a terrific profit overall. That is how Chipping works. The Chipper does not try to buy stock at the bottom and sell it at the top. Only Houdini could do that, and I'm not a Houdini and probably neither are you. As I write this today, GZMO stock is priced at $1.75. In other words, the buy and hold player missed the five-fold jump in value that I earned and he still holds the shares at the same price they were at nearly two year ago. I bought some back at $5.90 several months ago and more at $0.94 two weeks ago.

Before you make additional purchases at lower prices and accumulate a sizeable position in a company be totally sure that it really is a great company. Remember GZMO was a great company to me. I was willing to buy still more at $4 because I believed in its technological passion and was reassured by its financially strong parent (Genzyme Corp) despite its current lack of profits and limited sales. Sure things could have worked out differently and GZMO might have failed, but I had done a fair degree of homework and was comfortable with my assessment.

Use extreme care in selecting companies to buy. You may want to break your purchase choices into two groups: those that you are absolutely sure are great companies and those that you think are great companies. You should be willing to buy stock in the first group all the way down to a penny (obviously the stock of a great company never goes to $0.01 so think of this as just an expression). Companies in the second group can be re-bought if their prices fall further, but you might eventually have to decide with them that your "great company" decision was wrong, sell the stock and accept the loss.

Selling when the price rises is the key to the Chipping method. My GZMO examples notwithstanding, always take profits. You can't go broke earning 10% on an investment held for 2 weeks, a trade that translates into a 260% annual rate of return. The advice holds true even if the stock goes up a further 10% or even 100% more next week. A Chipper tries to repeatedly earn solid returns on many stocks held for relatively short time periods. Non-chipping investors worry about missing the next 10% run up in the price of a stock, never take profits and eventually wind up losers. Granted even confirmed Chippers have difficulty knowing when to sell. Suppose you buy a stock that was $20 per share yesterday for $14 a share today. A few days later it has risen to $15.25. Now what do you do? The answer depends on a lot of things: how is the overall market trading, how quickly did the stock bounce back, how many shares traded on the day that it fell, and does there still seem to be buying pressure? You will become a better seller with experience but remember you will be wrong about half of the time. That's OK what really matters is that you make enough profits on your trades to be a winner.

Lets talk some more about the hard part: when to sell. Tongue in cheek, let me say don't sell out too soon but never hold on too long. Advice like that is as useless as a parent warning their kids not to get hurt when they go out for a bike ride. Parents don't really believe that those words protect their kids but every parent says them. I suspect that in part they say them to assuage their guilt should something terrible in fact happen. I don't think my selling advice is similarly useless milksop. The selling advice translates into "don't let a good profit turn into a loss but try to sell out near the top." Obviously, no one can accomplish both goals simultaneously. A practical strategy sometimes is to sell a portion of your gains now and then sell the rest hopefully later after the price goes up further. An extra $5 or $10.99 commission is a fair price to pay for an extra $100 profit tomorrow. If your job permits, watch the stock's price frequently during the day (see the Yahoo discussion below in Appendix B) and try to discover if buyers and are pursuing the stock pushing up its price and where upward resistance occurs because sellers suddenly appear. Yahoo charts are especially helpful with this learning exercise.

The worst thing to be in the stock market is a follower because it is unlikely to result in you being a winner. Following someone else's purchase (sale) gets you in (out) too late. Chippers move against the tide but then try to ride on safe boats: great companies. Think about it rationally: why would someone give you, the small investor good advice? A friend on Wall Street says about the stock market: "Its all an information game." One way to interpret his comment is that throwing a dart at a newspaper's listing of stock quotations to find winners won't work; winners come from hard work and the diligent application of a sensible investing system. Where my friend and I disagree is in how much knowledge one needs and how much research is necessary. He is an old-line Wall Street type who believes in learning everything possible about a single company before investing even $1 in it. In contrast, I believe that it is possible to pick good stocks quickly – in as little as 15 or 20 minutes - after learning that their price has suffered a rapid decline following a not so bad news release; other more traditional investors, who would never Chip, would hotly dispute this basic Chipping concept. I discussed techniques designed to help identify great companies in Chapter 2. Chippers are leaders who take the road less traveled. While others are madly selling stock in great companies they are the buyers.

"EVERYONE KNOWS THE PRICE OF
EVERYTHING AND THE VALUE OF NOTHING"

The often cited but seldom attributed quote above belongs to the famous English bon vivant and author, Oscar Wilde. Study his words long and hard until you fully appreciate how within our society we always attach prices to objects that are desired such as stocks, real estate, art, and everything else without any concern for their true value. Some items are priced well in excess of their true value such as the latest fad in fashion or toys while others are priced below their value such as real estate in rundown parts of major cities.

Psychological barriers interfere with the typical investor's initial plans to try Chipping. The investor must destroy that emotional barrier using Oscar Wilde's words as a powerful ram. The first step to Nirvana occurs here. As you learn more about Chipping, keep thinking about the difference between price and value. What is the price of something? What is its value? Price, of course, is the dollar amount charged to buyers and given to sellers. But where does price come from? Value is what something is actually worth. But what is something really worth?

For hundreds of years, economists have studied markets and price formation. More recently, business school academics have considered the question of how companies set product price levels. Despite all this attention, the subject remains clouded in mystery. Certainly competitive markets with many active participants, uniform product characteristics, and perfect information are controlled by the miraculous powers of "supply and demand." But few markets are truly competitive and psychological factors including panics, bandwagons, and trends intervene and move prices to levels beyond what supply and demand alone would produce.

True value is even harder to explain than price level. Consider the extraordinary purchase by a Japanese corporation in 1990 for $82.5 million dollars of Van Gough's *Portrait of Dr. Gachet*. At that time, to that company, the painting had a value in excess of $82.5 million since that's what they paid for it. Thirteen years later the painting would probably fetch about $41 million at auction, which adjusted for inflation, is about $30 million in 1990 dollars. Its price has fallen by 64% in real terms while the painting itself has not changed one iota. But $30 million may not be its value. Philistines in our midst might argue that if you can't eat it, sleep with it, or produce something with it then it has no value. For them, a Van Gough painting is worthless. Strangely, the Japanese corporation may still value (emotionally not balance sheet wise) the painting at $72 million regardless of its current market price. Oscar Wilde might say that everything, including the painting, has a value that derives not from what you could sell it to someone else for but how much you would pay for it if you had no other information about its price or how others value it.

Buying a stock whose price has just plunged from $38 per share to $26 in a single day is an unusual strategy for traditional investors. The strategy is so unusual that when investors contemplate their first Chip they often decide not to proceed. To overcome this hesitancy, keep repeating Oscar Wilde's lesson and thoroughly understand this book. Something inside– self-doubt or a need to conform to "normal practices" - tries to convince you that this must be a dreadful company since its price just fell by $12 per share. Then you convince yourself that wiser people than you must know something that you don't know and you will not invest. That is how most people react. But if you believe that this is a great company and if you realize that $26 is just a number (in the form of a price) that cleared out today's supply and demand for the stock then you may overcome your metal restraints and buy it because you believe its value exceeds its price.

A perfect example of the price/value conundrum identified by Oscar Wilde is the history of the entire Internet sector during the turbulent 1998 – 2002 period. Some investors bought shares in Internet companies with prices in the $150 a share range and higher only because the price itself convinced them that the company had a future and they wanted to join the Internet revolution. Closer inspection reveals that these companies had flawed business models with breakeven sales 20 times their existing sales levels, and were able to attract customers only by giving their product away. In other words, they had no real value. A society that lets price determine value is prone to Internet stock fiascoes and more to the point here, teaches investors to eschew stocks whose prices fall precipitously. Now that some of these stocks are priced at $3 per share or lower, the same investors believe that they have no value. In most cases, this new insight comes from the price level and nothing more. In other words, it is as ignorant as was the earlier insight.

Think of Shares You Own as Inventory in a Hardware Store

The objective of investing is to make money. Agreeing with that statement leads to the next premise that says to make money you must buy stocks cheaply and sell them when they are priced dearly. That truism is business' most fundamental statement. Chipping merely operationalizes that concept for investors.

Take a stroll through a hardware store sometime and examine its myriad supply of goods. Then stand at the cash register and watch the sorts of transactions taking place. Many are the sale of four screws for $0.79 or a roll of tape for $1.29. How can this be a going business with low revenue sales occurring at a snail's pace? And a good business it truly is with multiple stores in every city and many families supported by the store's revenues. The key to the hardware business is the merchant's cost of inventory. The four screws cost in total about $0.11 while the tape cost $0.40. In other words, the firm's gross margin (price minus cost) is humongous. On screws the gross margin is 86%! Most successful businesses have gross margins between 25% and 50%. The key to the hardware store business is cheap inventory sold at a high price.

Chippers behave in the stock market like a hardware store. They buy stock in great companies after some news that has little long-term impact reduces its price and then they hold onto the shares until a buyer comes along willing to pay a higher price. Hopefully, the selling transaction occurs tomorrow or soon thereafter. If you are a Chipper you will not hesitate to sell at a good profit despite the nagging thought that "maybe the price will double or triple next week." Like the hardware storeowner a Chipper wants to get rich slowly on many small sales rather than on one gigantic profit from the next Microsoft. Rarely does the hardware store run out of inventory. Chippers may never fully sell out their inventory of stock in some great company whose trading pattern they have learned and whose price swings are wide and frequent. In a falling market the Chipper's current inventory of stocks may be comprised entirely of shares priced at less than her cost if as stocks fall she buys more shares on the way down. While this is not the preferred arrangement, it should not create too much concern, assuming that she has been taking profits too and that she has adhered to the rule to keep most of her funds in cash. These shares will be sold once their price rises to a point where she can sell them at a profit.

If you think the hardware store example is childish, consider this: underlying the order and certainty of the entire New York Stock Exchange is an individual called the specialist who does nothing more than what I have just described. She stands ready to make a market – buying or selling – a particular stock all the time. Usually, her bid and ask prices are what you see when you get a stock quote during trading hours. The specialist accumulates inventory when stock prices are falling and sells off inventory for a profit when prices are rising. Her stated purpose is to maintain an orderly market in a stock so that a relatively large buyer or seller will not momentarily disrupt the smooth operations of the market and the stock's price. While performing that task, she also trades for her own account and quite possibly profits on each transaction. Guess what: she's Chipping! If Chipping is good enough for the NYSE specialist then it is good enough for most investors. The difference between the specialist and the Chipper is that the specialist stands ready to make every trade on both the buy and sell side while the Chipper only wants to buy when the stock becomes a bargain because it has been unfairly penalized because of a news announcement.

Never Chase a Rising Target

Momentum investors chase stocks whose prices are rising. They look at the morning paper (or track stocks on the Internet during the day) to learn which stock had the largest percentage increase and then they buy that stock. Their plan is to catch a rising star on the way up. If that system works for you then forget Chipping and be a momentum investor.

Chippers take a different approach. They examine newspapers or midday quotes to identify stocks whose prices have declined the most. Finding a candidate they quickly work to determine if it is a great company.

Chippers never identify great companies based on previous high stock price. Price and value are not necessarily related. A $150 per share Internet stock now priced at $1 is probably not a great company though it may be. Factors to consider in deciding whether a company is a great company are is it a market leader (e.g., Microsoft or Motorola), a brand name (Kleenex or Kellogg's), the holder of special patents, mineral rights, or something else in scarce supply (Genzyme Corp) or a steady earner of corporate profits (Procter & Gamble). Chapter 2 discusses related issues. Since this search is done in real-time, rely heavily on Yahoo and other Internet sources for quick information retrieval.

Don't buy stocks that fall hard for no apparent reason. There should immediately be a news item on the Internet that "explains" the reason for the drop. If there isn't, ignore the company. Maybe it's just a large seller wanting out at any price but then again maybe someone knows something that not been released yet.

The size of the price decrement in a great company stock occurring in a single day following an unexpected bad-news announcement depends on investor psychology and the direction of the overall stock market. If the news panics investors the price may fall by 30 or 40% in one day. The very same information released instead on a day that finds investors in a calmer mood might produce only a 10% decrement. Another factor affecting the size of the price decrease following a news release is the market's overall trend. While markets are rising, small price declines, on the order of 10 – 15%, are more common. In market retreats anything is possible. The Chipper works with what is available. Bigger declines are better because it is more likely that investors have overreacted to the news. Profits can be made during both up and down markets though it is harder during the later and virtually impossible in a collapsing market. Stocks with bad news trade down precipitously on good days just as they do when markets are falling.

On March 2, 2001, with the NASDAQ down nearly 58% from its recent peak, I bought shares of Oracle, a great company, at $16.50 down about 33% from the prior day after it announced a modest sales slowdown in the current recession-like quarter. Less than a week later the stock was $18.50 providing a comfortable 12% return. The price of AOL Time Warner a company with a $95 billion market capitalization and $40 billion in annual sales fell by more than 10% between April 10th and April 11th 2002 because of analyst's concern about its Internet unit. By April 16th the stock had recouped the entire 10% loss. Appendix A presents other examples of successful Chips.

When reading this section in the future do not question whether the prices of AOL Time Warner or Oracle stock are higher on that day than the prices mentioned on this page. That's a buy and hold type question pertinent only to a long run investor. The Chipping question that you should ask is whether I made a profit.

Take Short Sizeable Gains Quickly

Sometimes everything goes right. A great company's stock is beaten down by 20% after a news release that has no long-term impact. Being a Chipper you pounce and buy the stock at the absolute low for the day and by market-close the price has recovered by 8%. The next morning the stock opens up another 4% and then stalls out. Your investment appreciated by 12% in little more then a day. Now what do you do?

Your first inclination will be to keep the stock and hope to make more money since this is a great company. While that may in fact be the right thing to do for this particular stock, my goal is for you to learn a system that may lead to profits from most good companies whose stock price declines. If this good fortune befalls you on your first Chipping investment, then you are poised to really decide what type of stock market investor you want to be: a Chipper or a buy-and-hold investor. Make a choice. Sophisticated investors can do both with different stocks, but until you become expert at Chipping, I recommend that you stick with one system. That way, you won't be confused and will know what to do with your 12% one-day gain. My recommendation in the "best of all world's scenario above" is sell the stock. Sure it may keep rising, but it may also go back down. Take your funds out and wait like a sneaky sand spider for your next victim to come along.

As your stock market prowess grows you may consider a mixed trading system wherein you hold onto some companies differently than others. My advice though is wait until you have mastered the Chipping system before you try to combine it with another system. After you acquire creditable Chipper skills there is no reason why after analytical scrutiny you can not treat a particular stock with great future potential differently and hold it long term. Coca-Cola in early 2000 is a good example of this. Coca-Cola meets almost all the requirements of being considered a great company. Slowing product sales and a product contamination scare in Belgium beat down the stock from $65 to $43 in that February to March period. There was money to be made Chipping Coca-Cola then: within six months it was back to $51. However, a compelling argument could have been made at that time to hold the position in Coke longer term. As it turns out, and yes I am using hindsight to create a perfect example, the stock increased nearly 50% more during the next half year.

For now, decide whether you are going to be a Chipper or a bottom-fisher that buys on deep-dips. Chippers have the discipline to buy stocks when other investors are rushing to sell and to sell stocks when other investors regain confidence and begin to buy. Bottom fishers simply buy low price stocks. Moving against the crowd is not easy: try doing that at a ball game or in a busy train station. It's the same way in the stock market. Stock prices are continually affected by new facts and how those facts influence investor psychology. Sometimes both factors work against a company causing its price to plunge. Provided that the new facts are not too material, Chippers gain from short-term changes in psychology. Chipping may be a system that will help you to profit on Wall Street. Until you prove to yourself that you have the discipline to be a successful Chipper, I recommend that you forget about doing several things at one time such as bottom fishing or following a buy-and-hold strategy and just work on making money quickly. If you prove inept at Chipping then drop it and return to some other strategy.

Undoubtedly, some companies that you Chip will continue to rise in price after they are sold. Although it is easy to focus on those securities and to ignore what you are achieving by Chipping, there are also companies whose prices decline after you sell them. To evaluate Chipping unbiasedly, do not let human nature lead you to ignore one type of after-sale outcome by focusing only on mistakes or victories; consider both types. Otherwise you will unfairly criticize yourself and will not be giving Chipping a fair test. Finally, if you think you should have held on to a stock that kept rising after you sold it, ask yourself when you would ever have sold it? My guess is that as a buy-and-hold investor you would have ridden it up to its new high, watched it decline again, and then still held it years later at about the same price or lower.

Getting Back Into the Saddle

Suppose that after selling the successful Chip described above in which you earned 12% in a single day that the price of that stock begins to fall again. What should you do? Lets bifurcate the situation into the possibility that a) the price plunges for a second time when further bad news comes out and b) it gradually falls at a pace of say ½ percent a day for several days. In the first situation, the pat answer is if the company is still a great company then of course buy it back. In fact, you might want to put all the dollars taken out after the first trade back into the company at its substantially lower price. Don't go overboard and think you have found the goose that lays the golden egg and put a lot more money into the stock. A key premise of Chipping is to control the investment size to avoid taking a big loss. On the other hand, be suspicious of a company that has more than one "startling" news announcement within a short time span. Companies generally are smart enough to dump all the bad news at one time. If for nothing else be suspicious because its management has not done a good job of managing the news. Perhaps management was so focused on the original problem that it overlooked the new problem. Maybe, but then you must worry that there may be more bad news coming that has also been overlooked. You would be wise to expend extra effort to consider whether this company is really great. To be extra cautious you might simply classify any company experiencing a double news whammy within a month or so as a bad Chipping candidate.

In the second event where the company's stock price gradually fads away, I am usually reluctant to buy it back again until it gets very close to or below the price that I originally paid after it fell sharply. The reason for this caution is to avoid trading stocks that are efficiently priced. For example, why did IBM stock go up or down by $0.25

today? It's not that anything fundamental has changed causing the market to revalue the firm 0.4% above or below yesterday's closing price. Using the parlance of academic finance circles is it possible that "its present discounted value of future cash flows has changed since yesterday by 0.4%?" The answer is obviously no. The reason why stock prices fluctuate in the short term is that today there are more buyers than sellers or vice versa: nothing more and nothing less. Chippers are not interested in buying stocks because the short-term trading activity of the past few days has caused prices to move slightly away from their "efficient level." They look for opportunities to buy stocks whose prices have moved a great distance from efficiency. Chipping is not like day-trading where an investor buys a lot of stock today and hopes that within a few minutes its price rises by a little bit. Chippers want to earn large percentage profits in relatively short time periods (days or weeks) on great companies whose shares they are not afraid to own.

If you are enticed to buy back a successful Chip a stock before it experiences another day of cataclysmically falling stock price, you have either fallen in love with the company or have succumbed to its familiar household name. In either case, your motives are suspect. Avoid being drawn back to a stock by its low price compared with its historic price. That is no reason to buy a stock. Price and value are not inextricably linked; they can deviate with price being above or below value.

Let me confess: I have repurchased companies like this one too but usually I can restrain myself until its price is at least below the price I originally paid. I then assure myself that the price is again inefficient, but that may not be true if months of trading have past. In retrospect, the immortal words of Thomas Wolfe, "You can't go home again," generally applies to ill-conceived repurchase decisions. More often than not, it has been necessary to buy the stock a second or a third time at a still lower price, after repurchasing it following a winning Chip. The lessons to learn are that it is very hard to pick a stock's bottom when it is trading along with the market as a whole. Notice the difference from Chipping. Also learn that stocks don't start to rise again just because you personally repurchased shares. That's simply wishful thinking.

Short Interest and Chipping

Investors short stocks by selling securities that they do not own. Their motivation is to profit from a future price decline occurring for any of a number of reasons. The shorted shares are borrowed through a brokerage firm from an investor who owns them. Generally short sellers are speculators who quickly cover (repurchase) shares sold short. For that reason, Chippers should review the short interest position (the total number of shares sold short) in a possible Chip before making an initial purchase. This data is available in Yahoo Profiles. The idea is that a stock with a large short interest position (many borrowed shares sold) is more likely to rise after a sudden price decline since short sellers may rush to cover (reduce) their exposure. Companies with low short interest positions can still be Chipped. In fact, great companies by their nature have fewer short sellers than do not-so-great companies.

Reverse Chipping is a related topic worth discussing in this short interest section. Sometimes a stock rises too much on not so great news. For example, a company might announce that it is submitting an application to the Food and Drug Administration to review a new drug. The FDA might in the future reject the application itself and even if it conducts the review might decide in a year or so that the drug is not worthwhile. Sure if this news was not already known the stock price should probably rise but by how much? Conceivably the stock may rise too much in which case a Chipper would consider shorting the stock in anticipation of a future price decline. Be warned! Shorting is dangerous since possible gains and losses are asymmetrically weighted towards losses and negative bets on a stock contradict most investor's ingrained optimism. Only sophisticated traders should short stocks. Few investors should try reverse Chips.

Chapter 6
Refining the Chipping Technique

HOLDING CASH CREATES OPPORTUNITY

Gamblers looking for "can't-miss winning strategies" eventually hit upon the "Doubling Up" theory. Probably few schemes have bankrupted as many intelligent people as that simple idea. Doubling up claims that you will eventually break the house (the casino) if you start with an infinite amount of money, bet solely on black at the roulette table and double your bet each time you lose. The theory is correct in the long run but false when the individual gambler tries it. The problem is that no one starts with an infinite amount of money nor does anyone live forever. Games of chance, and lets include the stock market for now, have odds stacked in the house's favor. As a result, the roulette wheel eventually lands on enough consecutive red or green numbers to bankrupt any bettor who consistently bets on black, even King Midas.

How does this apply to Chipping? The significance of doubling up for Chipping is that no matter how capable an investor is someday he will confront a string of dreadful bad luck. Most likely, that will occur in synch with an overall market downturn. On that day, unless you have retained a large supply of uninvested cash you will be unable to buy more great company shares at lower prices. You will have to stop Chipping. This section discusses the need for the Chipper to always maintain a cash reserve. Always means always! On the worst day of the worst bear market a Chipper still has cash to invest.

Deciding exactly how much cash to hold is a personal decision dependent on your tolerance for risk, wealth, and Chipping ability. Until you achieve proficiency in Chipping, limit your total Chipping investment pool to a small amount of money that you can afford to lose. After gaining confidence and some profits from preliminary Chipping activity, you may want to increase the funds in your Chipping business. Even then, your cash holdings remain important in terms of interest earned, future investment possibilities, and overall financial health. The following standard may guide your cash-balance target setting behavior.

Start by holding all of your investable funds as cash in an interest bearing brokerage account. Then begin Chipping but never let your cash holdings fall below the 80% level. That is, put no more than 20% of your funds into Chips at any one time. Naturally, these funds should be allocated across a number of different investments. How many are too few is subjective. I would avoid fewer than six and would not be uncomfortable with as many as 25 but certainly your degree of diversification is dependent, to an extent, on how much money 20% of your funds amounts to. Deviate from the 20% level only under two conditions: 1) you are profiting from 90% of your Chips or 2) the market sells off sharply. In the first case, it is not unreasonable to decrease your cash level to 70% by expanding the number of different companies whose shares are purchased when their prices are knocked down. Do not increase your investment level by buying more shares of individual companies. Chipping is about minimizing risk and putting "more eggs into one basket" increases risk. In the second case, once the market has finished its major downward move you might move 10-15% more of your fund into stocks and out of cash. You would then have a cash horde of about 65-70%.

Chipping requires quick decision making to assess whether a company is great. Though you will probably become better at making this assessment the more you Chip, it would still be imprudent to over invest in any one company unless you know something about it that others do not know. In my opinion, there is even excessive risk if you investment too much in any one industry. No matter how attractive the price of a company seems now, don't get sucked into buying too many shares.

If after using more of your cash you continue to profit from 90% of your investments don't decrease your cash horde any further. The only event that might push you to buy still more stock with cash would be if the market took a nasty fall. In that case, you might allocate another 10-20% of cash in stages into the market leaving your cash level at about 50%. If the market enters a bear phase (a decline in excess of 20%) you might even commit a further 20%. On the day that most analysts think that the market is at its bottom, you should have nearly 30% of your investment hoard still in cash. The reason is simple. Stocks always go up by more than you expect and go down by more than you expect. In other words, on the day after all the pro's on Wall Street think that the market has bottomed out, it will probably go down still further and you want some cash left with which to Chip.

Chipping requires flexibility and a continued ability to buy stock. Like a general who holds back his reserves so long that they are never committed to battle, always have plenty of cash left to buy great companies whose prices are beaten down to bargain levels. Remain patient. Don't rush to put money to work. This applies both to deciding which companies to invest in and exactly when to invest in them. Let me be emphatic on both points.

1. You are better off missing a great Chip because of extra time put into researching whether the company is truly great then buying beaten down shares of a not so great company.
2. If the market is falling or plunging, even great stocks that have been unfairly punished by bad news may have difficulty rising in price.

It is easier to earn Chipping profits in steady or rising markets.

Although hammered stocks follow no general rule or pattern, prices on the day after a bad news announcement might trace out a path similar to that described in Table 1 below. At the opening the price plunges. Then throughout the rest of the day the stock trades up and down as at one point more buyers push up the price and then later as more sellers push the price back down. Fundamentally, the price remains anchored near the opening level. For a minority of companies their stock price starts to recover near the opening bell at 9:45 a.m. or so. I usually miss out buying those cases and I don't mind. The rest tend to drift at the new lower price for at least a day. Some have a bad day at the start of the next day and then start to recover.

Table 1 A Possible Time Path for a Great Company's Stock Following a Not so Bad Announcement

Time	Price
Prior day closing	$50.00
9:30 a.m.	$37.00
9:40 a.m.	$34.00
9:50 a.m.	$35.00
10:00 a.m.	$37.00
10:10 a.m.	$38.00
10:20 a.m.	$37.00
10:30 a.m.	$37.00
...	...
3:30 p.m	$37.00
3:50 p.m	$36.50 or $37.50

Again referring to the table, I think the best time to buy a hammered stock is near 3:50 p.m. or on the second day after the price-affecting announcement. The objective is to wait until most panicked sellers dump their shares. Once it looks like the sellers have run out of steam, the time may have come to buy. The only guarantee that I can give you is that your timing will be wrong. It's impossible to time your purchases to pay the lowest price. Instead, hope to avoid overpaying by too much. When you do, say you buy at 3:55 p.m. at $38, and the stock trades the next day at $34, if you still feel it is a great company, you might then buy more. Notice again how important it is to keep your positions small. About half of the time that you buy, the stock will fall more afterwards. A further fall of 4-5% or more may be a wonderful opportunity to increase your position in a great company and to lower your average cost.

When buying and selling, real time quotes are an important tool to avoid jumping in too soon when the stock is poised to fall more. There are two types of real time quotes: Level I and Level II. Some Internet brokerage firms provide Level I quotes for free, a few give away both types, the majority charge for Level II quotes, while others charge for both types of quotes. Don't choose a broker solely on the basis of receiving free quotes: overpaying commission costs may overwhelm the gains from a free quote service. You might benefit from having two brokers: one who offers free trades and another who gives away free quotes.

Level I quotes, on a real-time basis, reveal the best sale price and the number of shares for sale and the best buy price and the number of shares available. For example, the Level I quote for a particular stock might be 1,000 shares offered to buy at $37 and 4,000 shares offered to sell at $37.01. With the boat tipped to the sell side this way, it appears that the stock is set to fall. However, the Level II quote, which reveals the size of other offers that are not the best, might show that there is a bid to buy 100,000 shares at $36.99. With that extra information, it appears unlikely that the stock will fall much more than a penny. If moreover, the Level II quote reveals that there are no sellers after the

4,000 shares available for sale at $37.01 until a 5,000-share block at $37.10 and a 3,500-share block at $37.18 it would seem that the stock is poised to rise.

Although the discussion above may sound a lot like day trading because of the detailed time and price information provided, that is not at all the case. As I've warned repeatedly, Chipping is not about buying large blocks of stock in one company and then selling them within minutes for a small gain. Yet the price paid influences the profits earned. Being circumspect in order placement can easily save a few pennies a share if not more.

NOW THAT YOU'RE EXPERIENCED

At this point lets assume that you have tried to Chip about 50 times over the last month or two. Additionally, assume that you did pretty well; maybe you broke even on the first 5 or 10 trades and then once you got the rhythm of Chipping you made money on about 35 out of the final 40 trades. If that is true then you are ready to consider more advanced Chipping issues presented below. Other less advanced readers should study this section now and also return to it in the future after they gain active Chipping experience. Finally, readers unsure of whether Chipping is for them should read this section for further reasons to give the technique a try.

Markets Go Up, Down, and Sideward

People entering the investment field during the 1990s succumbed to three demonstrably mistaken beliefs. The first is that stock prices always go up. Although the empirical evidence shown in Chapter 1 demonstrates that over a long time frame (perhaps decades from now) stocks are a good investment relative to other alternatives that does not mean that the prices of all stocks always rise.

What we really have is a market for stocks and not a stock market. The distinction is subtle but key to an understanding of the financial system, which is comprised of several markets where the securities of many companies are simultaneously traded. The rise and fall of individual stock prices causes the overall market to move. While historical evidence supports the argument that equities outperform other investments over the long run, it is a distortion of that theory to believe that any particular stock will rise if held on to long enough.

Not only may individual stock prices not rise, but Robert Shiller succinctly explains in *Irrational Exuberance* that a) markets are cyclical (they go up and down) and b) after falling, markets may require years or even decades to return to former heights. A simple examination of the Dow Jones Industrial average since 1930 reveals at least 20 instances during which this broad market measure has fallen for an extended time period: so much for the notion that stock markets always go up. Investors must never forget that markets go up and down, go up and down by more than they deserve, and can stay down for a long time. Even during falling markets some stock prices rise. Chipping candidates who have already experienced falling stock prices because of an announcement effect may be the best performers in a weak market.

Believing that stocks always rise led to a second mistaken belief: always stay fully invested in the market. This hallucination was institutionalized with the simple expression "buy and hold" and was emphasized by the derision of anyone who sold his Microsoft (fill in the blank with the name of any high flyer) shares too early. Instead, these sage minds should have said a) holding stocks through a market decline such as was experienced in 2000-2002 is irrational and b) finding another Microsoft is as difficult as predicting which team will win the pennant this year.

Investors falling for these first two mistakes received the coup de gráce when they made the ultimate mistake; they thought that the price of a stock was the same as its value. They forgot what Oscar Wilde said about cynics. Putting these three errors together -- markets always go up, always be fully invested, and high price equates to high value –money was invested in expensive stocks and left there. What a cruel triple whammy: stocks always go up, stay fully invested, and the more expensive the stock the better. People made money with those beliefs for a time, but eventually the truth prevails:

- stocks go up, down, and sideward;
- cash is king; and
- high priced stocks fall just as fast as do low priced stocks when they report unanticipated bad news.

Do you having trouble believe the first truth that stocks go up, down, and sidewards? Convince yourself of this by graphically examining the movement of any company's stock price on Yahoo finance or any of the other Internet based portfolio services. For example, bring your web browser to http://finance.yahoo.com/?u. From there the "Symbol Lookup" button will find the stock symbol of any company you are interested in. Once a stock price quote comes up look at the accompanying graph. For most companies, for any period longer than a single day or two the graph portrays the stock price moving both upwards and downwards. Stock prices virtually never go straight up or straight down; they just don't behave that way.

The fact that stock price movements do not track nicely along a straight line is not evidence that Chipping is a winning strategy. The almost random nature of stock price movements is merely a reflection of the fact that at various time there are more sellers than buyers and at other times there are more buyers than sellers. To base a strategy on the cyclical nature of stock price movements, in my opinion, is foolhardy since no one can pick the bottoms and tops of those cycles. Chipping involves something altogether different. Chippers buy stock in great companies after a market over reaction injures their prices following a not so bad announcement. They do not try to time the market. Chipping's objective is to seek out great stocks that have been excessively penalized.

A good example of a stock price overreacting to a lukewarm news announcement is what happened on April 19, 2002 to Vastera Inc. a small web-based software products and services company. While it is highly likely that Vastera is not a great company, what happened to its stock price that day is the archetype of what Chippers wait for. At 6:49 p.m. the night before, the company announced that it's 1st quarter 2002 net loss narrowed as revenue rose. Sales in the largest part of its business, managed services rose by 75 percent. Sales would have grown even more if its largest customer, Ford

Motor Company (nearly 37% of its sales) had not delayed a planned extension of its agreement to include Europe in addition to the company's current work in the US and Canada. The company's first-quarter net loss of $1.9 million compared very well against a prior's quarterly loss of $17.3 million. On a per share basis its pro forma operating loss of 2 cents per share was exactly equal to what analysts polled by Thomson Financial/First Call had expected. Furthermore, management remained upbeat. Mark Ferrer, president and chief executive officer said, "In the first quarter, we continued to execute on our strategy of expanding our managed services business geographically and vertically." Looking forward, the company said that it expected to have a 2nd quarter loss of 2 cents or possibly breakeven on revenues between $18.1 million to $19.4 million certainly in the range of 1st quarter revenues of $19 million. For the year it expected to have revenues of $80 million to $85 million.

The next morning a group of investment banks that followed Vastera including CIBC World Markets, Stephens Inc, Deutsche Securities and Jolson MP downgraded the company. The stock closed the night before at $11.25. After the news (hardly that bad) and the downgrades (overwhelming) the stock hit $5.53 at about 10:00 a.m. a decline of more than 50%. What is quintessential about the Vastera story is that on the same day that it downgraded the stock, Stephens Inc at 2:40 p.m. then upgraded the stock saying, "the stock is now oversold." The stock closed that day at $7.00. The point of the tale is not to buy at the low, $5.53, and then sell at the high, $7.00. Rather the point is that stock prices go up and down too much in response to news and that buying opportunities abound for those watching for overreactions.

The second great mistake that investors make is to constantly be fully invested. The opposing Chipping view is that "Cash is King." Sometimes this is expressed as "the Golden Rule: he who has the gold rules." Either way, the point is the same. Keep some of your powder dry. "Buy when you hear the cannons roar," the motto of the esteemed Rothschild family also plays upon the idea that cash is king. Their enormous family fortune was earned buying French government bonds at a few cents on the dollar when others were selling them in panic because the roar of the enemy's cannons could be heard in the distance. The prevailing story is that the Rothschilds used a new technology, carrier pigeons, to learn when the tide of battle had reversed before anyone else, letting them know that the value of the bonds far exceeded their price. Regardless of how they reached their buy decision, the family took advantage of the fact that markets overreact causing prices to fall or rise by too much and they had cash available. You might say that the Rothschilds were early Chippers.

Absent a crystal ball to predict the future, it is impossible to invest all your money at an individual stock's bottom. Likewise if you buy rising stocks (these are not Chipping candidates), the lack of clairvoyance leaves the investor prone to overpaying. No one can predict the tops or bottoms of individual stock or for the market in general for that matter.

Ordinary stocks fall for two reasons: a) due to market risk (the overall market declines and it pulls this stock down with it) and b) the release of an unexpected negative company news announcement. Chippers don't buy ordinary stocks because they try to avoid waking up in the morning owning a stock that has fallen by 25% since yesterday after a news release. Of course, even stocks that have just fall by 25% in a single day can still fall further. That's why it's so hard to buy at the bottom. When a stock that has been dramatically lowered in price is Chipped it probably retains a 50-50 chance of going up or down thereafter. Hopefully it will go up. But if it goes down, it is highly likely that it will fall by less than its initial decline. By keeping your initial purchase small (don't get carried away with what a great bargain this is) and maintaining a cash horde (CASH IS KING), you will be able to buy more of the stock at its lower price (perhaps 5-10% lower). Buying more at still lower prices gives you a chance to actually come close to buying some stock (not all your money) very near the bottom; in addition it will lower your average price and will let you operate your Chipping business as if you were the stock specialist who constantly makes a market for other investors in that stock.

High priced stocks can fall percentage wise in a single day just as fast as low priced stocks when unanticipated bad news is reported. Obviously, high priced stocks like Enron (once $80 a share) can plunge to mere pennies in a few

138

months when startling news seeps out. I'm not referring to that sort of situation. Chippers look for great companies that plunge (perhaps 20-30%) on a single day after a news announcement shakes the faith of investors who heretofore have believed in the company. Provided that the company is still great the post decline price is likely to be inefficient. Inefficient means that the price no longer fully reflects all the news that is available about the company such as its great management team, powerful new set of products, joint venture with a successful partner, new patent, limited indebtedness, etc. Instead investors focus on the immediate news that the CEO is ill or that the company now expects to grow at 8% versus the prior expectation of 9%.

If you are have trouble believing the basic idea that high priced stocks fall percentage wise as much as low priced stocks, then visit Yahoo's web page that reports the largest percentage changes in daily stock prices on the NYSE, AMEX and NASDAQ exchanges: its current URL is http://finance.yahoo.com/mnpl?e=NQ. Sure most of the spectacular flops are stocks priced below $10 per share but there are ample numbers of companies in these daily lists whose prices are in the mid teens and some in the twenties and higher. Although price does not denote value, companies priced at $20 after falling 35% in a single day are more likely to be great companies than those priced at $1.75 after falling by an equal percentage amount. Novice Chippers should probably never Chip any stock priced below $10 a share while expert Chippers should only do so once in a blue moon. Appendix A contains historic examples of great companies that provided Chipping opportunities.

My hope is that when financial historians revisit the precipitous meltdown of the high technology laced NASDAQ stock market that occurred in 2000 - 2002 they will conclude that it left behind a positive outcome; namely, the permanent elimination of the three twisted falsehoods -- stocks always go up, always be fully invested, and high price equates to high value. Survivors of that disastrous period learned agonizing but important lessons. Perhaps the most critical lesson is that a perpetually rising stock market is just a myth. Lets review the record of stock performance over the past eighty years. In a broad sense, the stock market

- melted down form 2000 to 2002,
- rose from 1982 through 2000,
- was flat from 1965 through 1982,
- rose from 1942 through 1965, and
- fell from 1929 through 1942.

Across the entire period from 1929 – 2001, the market rose. These broad characterizations probably contributed to the establishment of the three falsehoods that foreshadowed the excesses in the late 1990s and that culminated in the sharp market fall off in 2000, 2001, and 2002.

Broad-brush stroke generalizations obliterate the fine details that tell the whole story. During even periods of generally rising stocks, the market was laced with intervals of flatness (for example most of 1998) and declines (in October of 1987 the stock market fell more than 25% in a single day). Likewise, during secularly declining stock markets, there are periods of flatness and moments of rising stock prices. In other words stocks go up and down they don't just go up.

A by product of all this variability in stock prices has been the development of a number of investment concepts designed to capitalize on the fact that stock prices vary. These compete with Chipping. If one works better for you than does Chipping stick with it.

- Buying and holding stocks,
- Buying the laggards from last year's S&P 500,

- Buying stocks with low price-earnings ratios,
- Buying stocks whose dividends provide at least a 4% return, or
- Buying stocks displaying upward price momentum

In my view, many of these theories work well at times but then when you come to depend on them they fail. The catchphrase "even a broken clock is right twice a day" comes to mind when considering some of these investing paradigms. However, some are reasonable techniques that may benefit certain investors. No investment idea always works, not even Chipping. In my opinion though, the difference between Chipping, which seeks to buy great companies at a substantial discount and other investing systems is that if executed properly Chippers should be able to outperform the overall market in good and bad times because it reduces total risk by "removing or reducing" company risk and by confining itself to great companies. From my experience the annual rate of return earned by Chipping is higher during periods of rising stock markets then during falling markets. During most periods, that rate of return has the potential to exceed, on a risk-adjusted basis, what most investors earn elsewhere.

Vary Your Cash/Stock Mix with the Market Direction

As explained earlier, stocks face two major types of risk: one related to a particular company and the other aligned with the market. The former risk arises due to a company's actions such as an unsuccessful product introduction or the loss of a major contract. Chippers don't want to own stocks that have much company risk. Their

141

activities are confined to firms whose stock prices have already been pummeled by recent events. In that case, the firm confronts mainly market risk.

Market risk is the second type of hazard that investors are justifiably anxious about. It is the risk that the overall market will decline. The market panic in July 2002 (note market not company) when the Dow fell by over 25% in several weeks was an environment during which almost no one except a short seller could profit. Market risk is illustrated below using a twelve-month overview of changes in the Dow Jones Industrial Average and the NASDAQ average. Notice in Figure 1 how markets vacillate up and down in much the same way that individual company stocks do. Both broad aggregates in Figure 1, the Dow Jones Average and the NASDAQ, rise and fall repeatedly during a year. There are no long time spans during which markets just rise or fall continually. Movements in the overall market are like the ocean's tides; they pull most stocks along with them. Owning stocks while the market is retreating is likely to produce negative returns for the investor, this applies to the Chipper too when the market declines precipitously. In contrast, individual stocks tend to have positive returns when the market is rallying. A rising tide lifts all boats.

Most stocks go up while the stock market is rising. When the market is falling, most stocks decline. The "market" is a composite or average of many individual issues; naturally then the market is less volatile than some companies and more volatile than others. The finance profession has created a metric that compares how an individual stock's price movement compares with the overall market's moves. This metric is called beta or β. β is calculated statistically by comparing an individual stock's rate of return to the rate of return earned by the market. It describes a security's market risk and allows securities to be compared.

Companies which move at the market's pace both upwards and downwards are described as having a beta of 1.0. Owning a stock with a β of 1.0 should provide the investor with the same performance as she would experience if she owned a small amount of the entire market though company risk still exists. Index funds have βs very close to 1.0. Stocks whose movements are wilder than the overall market's reactions have betas greater than 1.0. A beta of 3.0, for example, means that when the market rises (falls) by 10% that this issue, based on prior performance, probably rises (falls) by 30%. Owning a high beta stock when the market is rising can produce high rates of return. But the beta relationship is symmetric; high beta stocks usually produce very negative returns when the market falls. Other stocks whose movements are less volatile than the overall market have betas less than one; these are relatively conservative issues. Stocks that move against the market have negative betas (i.e., they tend to go down when the market goes up and go up when the market goes down). Few stocks have negative betas.

Figure 1a The Dow Jones Industrial Average for the Twelve Months, October 29, 2001 – October 29, 2002

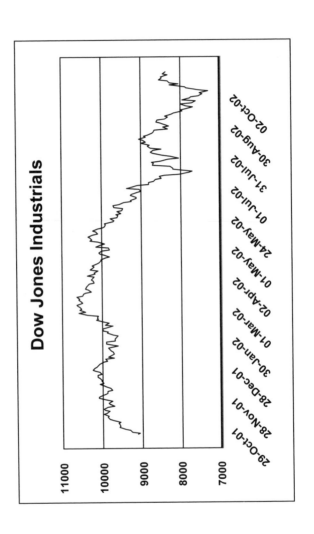

Figure 1b The NASDAQ Composite Average for the Twelve Months, October 29, 2001 – October 29, 2002

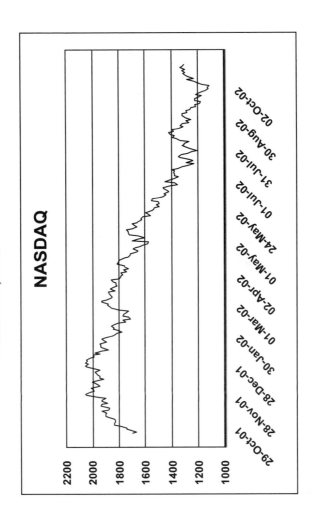

Stocks with high positive betas are often classified as aggressive assets while those with βs less than one are referred to as defensive assets. Aggressive assets have rates of return with more volatility (risk) than the market's return. Defensive assets have rates of return with less volatility than the overall market's return. A portfolio created by combing in equal proportion two assets with different betas has a portfolio beta that is effectively the average of the two company betas. This means, for example, that an investor who holds stock in the high β company where she works can neutralize the market risk in that position by creating a portfolio that includes an equal investment in a defensive stock.

The reason for mentioning the concept of betas is because investors need to be aware of how various stocks have differential degrees of volatility relative to the market. Every company's beta is obtainable via Yahoo Finance by first requesting its stock price quote and then clicking on the profile button followed by the ratio comparison button. It is not unreasonable to expect a high beta stock to bounce back more quickly after a punishing day of trading following a negative news announcement. However, if the stock's trading dynamic changes after the bad-news announcement, the beta might change too! Keep betas in the back of your mind; they should influence but not shape your Chipping activity.

Suppose you buy shares in a great stock that has been beaten down by bad news. The question to ask is can the stock's price recover a portion of its lost value even when the overall market declines. My own observations suggest that the answer to this question is yes provided that the overall market does not implode. Exaggerated pessimism that sweeps investors during a market route appears to reduce if not negate the quick recovery earned by beaten-down stocks. In contrast, ebullient markets experiencing a rally seem to allow beaten-down stocks to achieve a greater and more rapid price recovery. How should a Chipper take advantage of these observations? First, they should reduce the size of new positions taken in great companies during periods of market weakness. This strategy enables them to buy more of the shares if they track the overall market downward. Second, Chippers might modestly increase the size of new stock positions purchased during strong market periods. If a reasonable sized investment given your portfolio is $1,000 then during weak market periods this amount might be reduced to $800 or so while during exceptionally strong market periods this amount might grow to $1,200.

With all this discussion of markets in general, don't get caught up in market sentiment. Don't try to be a market timer. Your objective as a Chipper is to buy great companies cheaply and then sell those securities to someone else soon and make a healthy profit for your efforts. Let the market go up or down as it wishes. Just keep in mind the fact that like the tide, a falling market pulls and tugs a beaten-down stock reducing its ability to bounce back from its recent troubles.

AT THE BOTTOM STOCK UP AND SLOW DOWN YOUR SALES

Read the next section with caution and don't let it radically change your trading mechanics. Supposing that you've Chipped your way through a period of falling stocks and have finally arrived at the next expansionary period with more money than you started with, should you continue doing what you have been doing or make changes? A few simple adjustments may be in order now that the market is rallying again. First, it may not be unreasonable to increase your profit targets. If in the months preceding the bottom you took quick profits of 5 or 10% you may now be able to wait a bit longer and take profits of 10 or 20%. Second, it may be time to put more of your cash to work buying stock in more great companies whose shares have been beaten down. How much more money to invest is discussed more fully above. But the only way you should ever invest all of your cash in great companies is if a higher authority issued an absolute guarantee that the market will rise. Otherwise, no matter how confident you are that the bottom is just around the corner, you likely face disappointment. Realistically, you will never get such a guarantee of a bottom so always maintain a strong cash position. Several obvious warnings are in order:

1. Don't be a pig and allow good profits to become losses,
2. Don't try to call the market bottom yourself. Being the first person to call a bottom gains you little but being wrong on that call will cost you a lot.
3. Don't concentrate your money in a small number of stocks in case they still retain some company risk. Spread your funds around. Avoid concentrating your investment in one industry or related industries too.
4. Maintain some cash so that if the market has not bottomed you can keep on Chipping.

These four caveats are discussed below.

Avoid the Pig Farm

The reason to worry about visiting the pig farm is that there are many false bottoms during every market decline. Listen to the following scenario to see how a false bottom can occur. Stocks start to rise for some reason; maybe short sellers need to cover their positions on a certain day. Other investors notice the rise and jump in thinking there may be some upward momentum that they can draft on. The overall movement in stocks gives optimism to others who then purchase shares themselves. The market has now risen maybe 10% or so. Suddenly, the buyers dry up as more negative news filters out and stocks start to slip down again. In this scenario, pigs (not Chippers) soon own a portfolio of stocks on which they had gains but did not sell that are now all losers. If this happens to you, and I admit that it has happened to me, you quickly reconsider the philosophy of Chipping.

Yet despite the scenario recounted above, try to hold on for more profits when the market is running upwards. As stated in Chapter 2, knowing when to sell is harder than having the smarts to buy after a great company rings a loud bell and says the CEO just quit. If the market is doing nothing only moving sideward a quick 5-10% jump in a beaten-down great company is adequate, but when the market is frothing upwards you may be able to do a whole lot better than 5%. Learn from your mistakes. If you take a quick 10% gain and the stock goes up 10% more before falling back, then don't stop Chipping and revert back to your old loser ways, but instead on your next Chip consider holding on a bit longer.

Closely watching winners that are ready to be harvested during the day may achieve a higher sales price though it is not easy to pick the top. Don't expect to be absolutely successful. Accept small victories like making an extra 10 cents per share because you held on for an extra 15 minutes. Moreover, busy people probably don't have time to constantly watch their stocks. What I do when I am ready to sell is to track real-time bid and ask prices looking for the immediate term weight of buyers versus sellers. There are no real secrets here just common sense. When there are 10,000 shares to buy and 100 for sale the stock usually goes up in price. If the stock then rises by 10 cents and the bid is still for 9,000 shares and the asked is only 200 shares, the price is likely to keep on rising. But it may not. Investors without Level 2 stock access (I don't have it yet) are at a disadvantage because they do not see that there are 400,000 shares to sell at a five-cent higher price. While most of us are disadvantaged because we don't have Level 2 screens, nonetheless, you can often avoid selling a stock too soon by watching the bid/ask size. Another way to try and sell a winner is by placing a limit order at a price several percentage points above its current level. The risk is that the stock falls before it reaches that price.

Now for a warning, not only is stock watching a time consuming and highly addictive activity but it is also highly speculative and non scientific. That's because it's a big market out there and you are only seeing a small piece of it. You may decide after watching for a few minutes that a stock has run out of gas and then sell it. 15 minutes later you may be anguished to see that it started to go up again. Perhaps what you saw was that a big buyer had pulled away from the market for a few minutes to see how the price would react. Or possibly a new buyer jumped in. Although this sounds a lot like day trading, it is not. All I'm suggesting is that you incorporate bid/ask information into the decision process of when to sell. Using my grocery store example, its no different than saying that you should buy chicken breasts at the store having the best sale price. Sell your stock at the highest price possible.

MARKET BOTTOMS MAY BE QUICKSAND

Wall St. pays its stars among the highest salaries in the world. Top performers take home astronomical pay packets of $10 - $15 million and super performers earn in excess of

$100 million. Salaries like these almost make the whopping money given to sports heroes look like chump-change. And yet these icons are generally unwilling to forecast a market bottom any further ahead than saying, "OK this is it. The market bottomed last month." That's not much of a forecast. You'd think these high priced experts could issue statements along the lines of "the market will bottom in three weeks and two days."

If major investment firms and top analysts hesitate to stake their reputations and money on a projection of when a market will bottom out, that's obviously not a territory that a rational person would want to put themselves into either. Let the market itself tell you when it has reached bottomed.

DON'T CONCENTRATE YOUR INVESTMENT IN A FEW COMPANIES

In addition to the risk avoidance reasons mentioned above for not holding too few companies in a portfolio, there is an additional problem with a lean portfolio when talking about market bottoms. When the market finally does recover having a thin portfolio may result in there being no winners in the group. While it is true that once the market starts to go back up most stocks rise, it is also true that the right stocks rise spectacularly. Portfolios with too few individual companies in them may have concentrated their holdings on the last expansion's leaders. Those companies may not be in the vanguard of the next boom. What you want to avoid is being left behind with a portfolio containing too few names.

Hold Some Cash to Keep on Chipping

Investing is not like the Charge of the Light Brigade or Custer's Last Stand where your last troops are thrown forward in the valiant hope of victory. In those historic situations, the commanders had no other choice but to gamble with everything they had. Only a foolish investor would put forth his last dollar of reserves hoping that the market had bottomed out. Investing gallantry has never been awarded a posthumous medal, songs are not composed, and Earl Flynn is not available to play you in the movie version. Always conserve cash. It is better to be a cautious winner rather than a reckless loser.

As discussed above, there is no compelling reason why markets must go up; downturns need not turnaround and become expansions. The Chipper's salvation in a down market is that she owns a portfolio of great companies whose shares were purchased cheaply, at least relative to where they had been before their startling announcement. Even during protracted periods of a down market, shares of these great companies sans their company risk should perform well relatively to the rest of the market.

More On Market Bottoms

Market cycles are amazing phenomenon to observe historically but painful to experience on the down swing. Looking back it appears that the investor can buy near the bottom and sell near the top but that degree of finesse is nearly impossible without there being a clear signal that a turning point has been reached. Moreover, is a turning point in one market, say the Dow Jones Industrials, related to the turning point of another market say the NASDAQ? The graph in Figure 2 overlays the two markets across a two-year time span. The data are presented as percent changes because the sizes of the two markets are radically different: the level of the Dow Jones Industrials is about five times higher than the NASDAQ. The starting point is October 29, 2000 and the graph ends two years later on October 29, 2002. The graph depicts the cumulative change in index values from October 29, 2000. Thus, the value on October 29, 2001 (365 days later) is the percentage change in an index from the prior year.

Figure 2 The Cumulative Percent Change in the Dow Jones Industrial Average and the NASDAQ Composite Average from October 29, 2002 through October 29, 2002

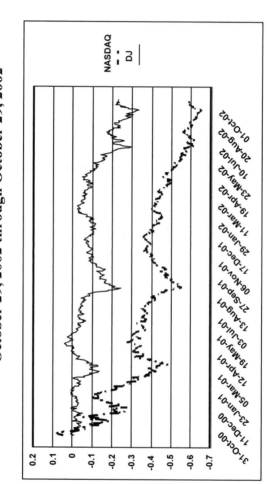

In addition to revealing the presence of cyclicality in both markets, the table demonstrates that the two markets follow similar patterns (rising and falling at about the same time) though with different percentage amplitudes. That is, both markets change direction on about the same day but the amount by which they move is unequal. For example, the NASDAQ fell about 60% from its July 2000 peak through April 2001; in contrast, the Dow fell by less than 20% during the similar period. The parallelism between the markets is imprecise but regular. Clearly, stocks, markets, and assets in general move to some degree in tandem but their paths are not inextricably linked.

Two ideas expressed earlier can now be interrelated. The first is the existence of market and company risk. The second is the idea of there being both a stock market and a market of stocks. The presence of company risk makes a monolithic stock market an obviously false construct. Certain stocks move independently of the market. These independent spirits have better or worse news than the rest of the market. Chippers buy those that are great companies following the release of bad news that beats down the price. Market risk exists and in part that what drives the overall stock market.

HOW LOW CAN MARKETS GO? HOW LOW CAN STOCKS GO?

The answer to the questions framing this section is simple: all the way to zero. How likely is it that markets will go to zero? The answer to that question is also easy: never! If the stock market were going to totally wipe out, it would have happened during the great depression that began in 1929 and that lasted for ten years. Times have changed since the 1930s and numerous developments have improved market resiliency. For example, in 1934 the Securities and Exchange Commission was created to help protect investors, also during the 1930s Federal Bank Deposit Insurance ended runs on banks, Regulation T gave the Federal Reserve the power to limit margin stock buying, and in 1972 floating currency exchange rates resumed. Concerning more recent dangers, computer programmed trading was restricted, the quality of accounting reports issued by companies have been improved by the Financial Accounting Standards Board and with the passage of the Sarbanes-Oxley Act of 2002, and reduced trading commissions and Internet brokers have enabled millions of investors to buy and sell securities more easily.

So how bad was the market during the depression? The answer is real bad. From its peak in 1929 at 381.17, the Dow Jones Industrials fell to 198.69 or by 48% in 1929 and to 41.22 or 89% at the trough in 1932. The Dow Jones Industrial's decline of 39% in 2000 – 2002 pales in comparison with these figures. The NASDAQ's decline of 79%, from peak to trough, is close enough to the Dow's experience during the depression to say that the high technology sector's market experienced a depression in 2000 – 2002.

It is noteworthy that before hitting its true bottom in 1932, the Dow Jones Industrials registered six false bottoms between 1929 and 1932 when the market rallied only to fall back again. It has never been easy to pick bottoms. Chipping's advice to sell winners may help the investor during future false bottom periods.

Bear in mind several thoughts about these data. First, markets can fall precipitously after reaching their peaks. That fact alone would seem to be sufficient reason to forestall anyone from ever adopting a buy-and-hold strategy. Second, where and when the market will bottom is unknown. Consider the six false bottoms and subsequent

156

short-term rallies during the depression. Buyers during those rallies regretted their decisions shortly thereafter. A Chipper, on the other hand, would never have held on until the interim peak that occurred between the two market bottoms because she would have sold out well before that time. Of course, she would have repurchased shares at some point while the market was approaching its next bottom.

When markets fall like a rock over a number of days or weeks, market risk outweighs company risk. The basic idea behind Chipping is that total investment risk can be reduced by buying companies with diminished company risk following the release of not so bad news about them that the market takes too hard. Periods of heightened market risk escalate the total risk of buying any stock, even a great Chip. At such times it may be wiser to wait until market turmoil subsidies and total investment risk is reduced. Market sages articulate this idea with the expression, "never try to catch a falling knife." What this means is that the market is likely to keep falling when that's its momentum and that you can hurt yourself badly if you try to time the market. Chippers are not market timers. They want to buy stocks that are inefficiently priced too low and sell them when they recover a part of their losses. A flat or rising market is the preferred time to Chip since in those cases the market is working in the Chippers favor.

The answer to how low individual stocks can go is completely different than the explanation provided above for markets. Individual stocks can and do fall to zero. Companies go bankrupt every day and in most of those cases the shareholders are left with nothing but memories. That is why an earlier warning suggested that you seriously review your great company call before repurchasing a stock that has fallen more since you first bought some of its shares. Hopefully, it won't happen frequently, but sometimes you should sell your position at a loss because you mistakenly bought a not so great company's stock.

HOW LONG DO YOU WAIT TO BUY?

No one can accurately pinpoint when to buy or sell. That decision rests on the investor's shoulders. She should know though that she will rarely be completely "right." If this makes you uncomfortable, then perhaps mutual fund investing is for you. Chapter 7 talks about Chipping mutual funds so don't stop reading. One thing is certain though: you will not consistently be able to buy at the bottom and sell at the top whether you buy stocks or mutual funds. That just can't be done. What you need is a plan to follow that helps make those decisions.

If you become a Chipper the plan is the same whether markets are rising or falling: buy great company stocks after they have been bashed down by unexpected bad news that in your opinion is not catastrophic. The idea is that markets are basically efficient (stocks are generally priced right), investors drive stocks up too much and down too much on the basis of news thereby making them inefficiently priced, and great companies survive even the worst of times.

CHIPPING IN FLAT MARKETS

Whether markets are rising, falling or going sideward, the Chipping Theory is based on the following scenario:
1. You buy shares in a great company after its price falls substantially following a news announcement that you don't feel was really that bad.

158

2. The stock is drained of virtually all company risk leaving you to worry only about market risk.
3. The stock is now priced inefficiently so that it should perform better than the overall market even during a period of market decline as its price returns to an efficient level.
4. When the stock rebounds, take profits and look for the next Chipping opportunity.

During flat markets, individual stocks go up and down while the overall market remains caught in a windless Bermuda Triangle. Flat markets may actually be the best times to Chip because if stocks are not being influenced much by market forces, other investors may more quickly perceive the inefficiency in the pricing of the great company, creating new demand and a higher price for the shares.

Might there be times when you would be better off not holding any stocks at all? Sure, if you know with certainty that the market is about to plunge, go to cash and wait there until the markets are ready to recover. Do such times every come? Rarely, but I suppose in retrospect the NASDAQ at 5,000 up from less than 500 in 1990 was such a time.

Chapter 7
Chipping Mutual Funds

Mutual funds, as discussed in Chapter 1, invest money for individuals for which they receive fees and expense reimbursement. Among the most common fees are loads (charged as a percentage of the investment like traditional brokerage commissions), 12b-1 fees collected annually to pay marketing and distribution expenses, and expense fees (to cover operating costs). Be careful when buying what are termed "no load funds" because some charge 12b-1 fees of as much as 0.25%. In addition, some mutual companies impose early redemption fees when funds are withdrawn before a certain amount of time elapses, low balance fees when the investor's holdings fall below a certain level, and some funds may limit the number of times a year that an investor can withdraw money. The average total fees paid to stock funds is about 1.5% per year while for bond funds it is about 1.0%. What the investor principally receives from paying these fees is professional money management.

Unlike individuals, investing is a full time occupation for most mutual fund portfolio managers. Their principle function is to choose which securities to buy for the portfolio and to decide when to sell those already owned. Most have earned MBA degrees from business schools and many are Chartered Financial Analysts (CFAs). Their knowledge of business and economics exceeds what the average investor knows. Some portfolio managers outperform their peers by earning higher returns on their investments though extending the comparison across a number of years significantly reduces the number of star mutual fund mangers. Some observers argue that funds cannot beat the market for an extended time period and therefore the accumulation of fees and expenses that they impose result in investors being worse off than if they invested on their own.

Fund management companies actually own mutual funds. Some companies own just a single fund while others own dozens of funds. Management companies are a business. They are interested in maximizing the money under management since their revenues equal a percentage of the total amount invested in the family of funds. Fund families such as Fidelity, Morgan Stanley, and Putnam attract new investors by offering a large variety of funds, excellent customer service, and convenient deposit and withdrawal mechanisms. In addition to these characteristics, Vanguard Group attracts new money by keeping its expenses low hoping to profit from a larger total volume of funds.

Certainly an important way to distinguish between funds is to compare the returns they earn. Several outside companies including Morningstar Inc. and Lipper Inc. compile and rank fund performance. Funds are first categorized based on their investing objectives. Then they group funds using devices such as star-rating systems that range between a one for low performance to a five for top performance. Many investors choose between funds based on Lipper or Morningstar ratings. To some extent these ratings are disingenuous. One technique that fund families utilize to maintain good ratings is to merge losing funds into other funds in the family or by shutting losers down altogether. This tactic erases losers from their list, and if small funds merge into larger funds may hardly detract from the overall performance of the larger fund. David Dreman confirmed this when he discovered that only 30 out of 220 funds in Lipper's Equity-Income category in 1988 were still around in 2001[25]. The other 190 funds had either merged within the family or had been liquidated.

---

[25] "Inefficient Market," David Dreman, Forbes, August 6, 2001, page 105.

Funds range in size from the tiny (such as the Valley Forge Fund a thirty-year-old fund that has less than $8 million) to the gargantuan (the Vanguard 500 Index Fund has over $90 billion in 2002). Small funds probably cannot offer the security coverage and research detail that larger funds provide. On the other hand, small funds can invest more nimbly and in smaller situations where larger funds are precluded. Investors are probably best served in the mid range of funds thereby avoiding the high expenses and low service of smaller funds and the limiting nature of larger funds. It has been argued that returns are related to the length of time that a manager is resident at a fund[26]. While these results are not overwhelmingly strong, it probably does not hurt when a manager has had a long tenure with a fund.

When choosing between mutual funds be aware of several things. First, fund names identify investment style. The Fidelity Technology Fund, for example, invests in technology stocks while the Wells Fargo Small Cap Growth Fund invests in small growth companies with low market capitalizations. Effective July 2002 the SEC requires funds to adhere to an 80% rule, which as its name implies requires that a fund hold 80% of its investments in securities that conform to the style indicated by its name. The prior rule allowed funds to hold just 65% of their assets in the category associated with the masthead. This rule helps investors to understand how a fund invests.

Equally helpful in picking funds is a matrix like that in Table 1 that some funds use to pictorially depict their investment focus. The fund described in the figure invests primarily in midrange-sized companies that, in the manager's view, are either undervalued or high growth vehicles. Investors can double-check this description with a

---

[26] "Older Managers Know funds Best," John Waggoner, USA Today, Internet Version, February 11, 2002.

short delay of a month to a quarter by viewing the top portfolio holdings of most funds at the funds web site or at Yahoo's mutual fund section. The matrix in Table 1 together with the "truth in labeling" required by the 80% name rule helps investors put their money into funds that conform closely to their investing wishes. Funds also issue highly informative prospectuses but few investors actually read them.

Table 1 Investment Focus

	Value	Blend	Growth
Large Capitalization			
Midrange Capitalization		▓▓▓▓▓	
Small Capitalization			

Second, funds regularly distribute dividends and capital gains to investors often in December. This is an especially irritating feature. Consider an investor who puts her money into a fund the month before its annual distribution date, for example, in November 1999. If the fund gained 75% during 1999 the investor would need to report those gains on her 2000 income tax despite the fact that the fund ended the year 2000 at a price below what she paid for it the year before. This anomaly occurs because funds are required by law to annually distribute to their owners 98% of their earnings, dividends and capital gains, so that funds not become tax havens. Providing some conciliation to the investor, her basis, or cost of acquiring the fund, is simultaneously reduced by the reported capital gain. However, the investor pays a tax on a capital gain that she never personally earned while savings from the lower basis

163

may nor may not counterbalance the current year's tax effect.

Finally, ignore the heavily promoted returns that fund families prominently display in their ads. What matters to investors are the after tax and after load net returns that can be found in the fund's prospectus. No-load funds have an advantage in this derby as do funds that retain their holdings long enough to avoid short-term capital gains taxation. There are no Chipping funds, as this is written though some have informally moved in that direction[27]. It has not been shown how a fund that takes quick profits from Chipping would compare on an after tax basis against an index fund like the Schwab 1000 Fund that buys and holds. Another reason to ignore mutual fund ads is that they promote past performance. The past and the future may bear little or no resemblance to each other. Stocks go up, down, and sideward and funds do too. That's why it is possible to Chip funds.

Recently, exchange traded funds (ETFs) have been created as alternatives to mutual funds. They appeal to investors who want the benefits of diversification but do not want to turn the management of their money over to someone else. ETFs are listed mainly on the American Stock Exchange and come in many forms including broad stock indexes and portfolios specific to industry, company size, and investment style. The largest are the NASDAQ-100, which includes the largest 100 technology stocks (stock symbol QQQ) and a S&P depository receipt tracking the S&P 500 (stock symbol SPY). Compared to mutual funds, ETFs have several advantages:

- They can be purchase in lots as small as a single share (often $30 or less).

---

[27] See Aaron Lucchetti, "Mutual fund Seeks tiny Gains in Many Trades," *Wall Street Journal*, July 23, 2002, page C1.

- They can be purchased during the day rather than after the market closes at 4:00.
- They can be purchased on margin or sold short.
- They do not charge management fees. Expenses are charged but these are relatively low (well below 1.0%).
- Capital gains are not distributed to ETF holders.

Throughout the remainder of this chapter the term mutual fund and ETF are used interchangeable.

AFTER THE HERD MOVES PICK UP THE PIECES

Mutual funds are agglomerations of individual stocks. While some funds hold as few as 25 stocks in their portfolios, most hold hundreds of issues. Even when a fund concentrates its capital narrowly on a single industry or country, the mutual fund portfolio faces less company risk than would an investment in a single company provided that the fund limits its investment in any one company. Consequently, funds have lower price volatility than individual stocks. That is a boon to investors while markets are falling but reduces mutual fund returns during rising markets. Of course, market risk equally affects mutual funds and private investors.

How then can mutual funds be Chipped? The question arises because mutual funds reduce company risk and if it is that loss in pricing efficiency that Chippers seek to take advantage of is there any inefficiency left for them to benefit from? The answer is that mutual fund mispricing occurs less often than for individual stocks but it does occur. Good stocks to Chip can be found every day or two or certainly more than once a week. Some Chips are better than others but in our dynamic world, things change quickly and markets move decisively when they do. In contrast, mutual fund Chips come less frequently maybe only several times a year. Before a mutual fund is ready to be Chipped the price of nearly every company in its portfolio must be decimated. This happens less often for generalized growth funds. However, the market can be quite finicky and decide that a particular industry or country is no longer a worthy investment. Country/region specific and industry-focused funds are where the Chipper seeks opportunity. It happens regularly, but not every day. When it happens, most stocks in the portfolio are inefficiently priced. More importantly, moods on Wall Street are temporary and what was despised lat year may be highly sought after this year. When that juxtaposition occurs, the mutual fund regains its efficient price level and the Chipper sells out.

Lets review an example of an industry shift that created inefficiencies in the pricing of securities in a particular narrow market. One already discussed above is the technology bubble that burst in 2000-2002. Today most investors are shunning the technology sector and some of those stocks are selling for little more than their net cash positions (i.e., the cash that would be left after selling off the business and paying down its debts). In other words, the market is valuing the fundamental business at zero! Several years ago, people would have laughed at the proposition that the technology sector could ever tumble so low. They were wrong. Similarly, people not buying into technology today are also wrong. I can't predict which stocks will rise but undoubtedly the whole sector will come up from these low levels. Mutual funds are perfect ways to speculate in a market like this where the pricing becomes inefficient.

Similar boom-to-bust cycles regularly affect the oil and gas, chemicals, paper, and durable goods stocks to name just a few. Wise observers know that investors rush headlong into sectors that have already experienced improvement thereby driving their prices up still further.

When circumstances reverse themselves in those industries, equity prices start to fall and investors shocked because prices don't go up forever dump the stocks and drive their prices down too far. What the Chipper wants to do is to wait for the dust to settle, move in, and make a profit.

But mutual funds are not the same as individual stocks and the rules that apply to Chipping mutual funds are not exactly the same as those used on stocks. In case you've forgotten lets review the five fundamental rules of Chipping:

- Only buy stocks of great companies.
- Wait to buy one until its price is dramatically reduced by a not so bad announcement.
- At first buy a relatively small amount of stock.
- If the price goes down still more and it remains a great company then buy more.
- If the price rises quickly, by about 10% or so, sell the stock.

In order to Chip mutual funds, these rules need to be adjusted. Lets go through them one by one and see how they change for mutual funds.

Replace the phrase great companies in the first rule with great industries or great countries. In other words, look for industries or countries which will be long-term winners and whose equities are priced below an efficient level as a consequence of misplaced investor psychology or overblown investor fear. These opportunities rarely come overnight as they do with stocks. Countries do not report that their GDP rose by 3.2% while analyst had expected 3.3% and then have their equities fall by 15% across the entire market in a single day. Similarly, sector funds that invest in single industries rarely fall by double-digit amounts instantaneously even though some individual stocks in the portfolio may move by that amount. Diversification provides benefits even when a portfolio is confined to a single industry.

167

The basic idea behind Chipping applies whether the security is an individual stock or a mutual fund representing a collection of stocks in a single industry or in a particular country or region. Mutual funds Chippers look for funds that have been dramatically reduced in price after an entire sector or country has fallen out of favor with investors. When investors panic and rush headlong away from a particular industry or country very often their motivation is simply to follow the crowd. Panics unjustifiably pummel stocks in an industry or country causing prices to fall to levels that are too low. Of course, just because a mutual fund's price is lower than it had been does not mean that it is a Chipping candidate. Before Chipping establish that a fund is concentrated on a narrow investment sector and that the sector is likely to be a long-term winner despite its current situation.

The best mutual funds to Chip are confined to specific industry sectors, countries, or geographic regions such as Southeast Asia or Latin America. As I've already said a number of times, stock prices decline for two reasons: market and company/country risk. It is more likely that price declines in a specific industrial sector result not only from market risk - a general decline in most stocks - but also from the accumulation of specific company risks. Stock prices of firms a single industry might decline more precipitously than other stocks as a result of macroeconomic factors (e.g., construction stocks move down when interest rates rise), environmental concerns, or shifting consumer tastes. Similarly, stocks in a particular country may decline more than world stock indices when bad economic policies alter the country's competitive position. Though imprecise, the investor can gauge the degree of overselling by comparing a mutual fund's decline to the overall change in the US market. For example, there is a stronger chance that overselling has occurred if an industry focused fund is down by 30% while the US market is down by 10% than if the US market were down by an equal amount.

In the second rule, replace the phrase "until its price is dramatically reduced by a not so bad announcement" with "until the fund's price has fallen substantially because virtually all of the stocks in the portfolio have been hammered relentlessly." It's far easier to know when an individual company's price is inefficient following a tepid announcement that literally kills the stock than to know when a fund is ready to Chip. Fund prices generally don't move as radically as do individual stock prices. But funds are aggregations of individual stocks and if a particular industry or country experiences a long string of bad news, the constituent stocks in the portfolio will eventually all be battered too. That is when you want to start to Chip. A telecom fund in mid-2002 would be an example of a possible fund Chip. Your timing will probably be worse when trying to Chip country funds because of the lack of the not so bad announcement effect and because you probably are more ignorant about the political and economic changes occurring in a country than you are about facts concerning a single company.

The third and fourth rules need no adjustment in order to apply to mutual funds. In fact, what they need is emphasis. Buying a bundle of stocks held in a mutual fund means that separate balance sheets or income statements are not analyzed, instead the investor is buying into a concept. Bottom fishers also buy mutual funds when they are down thinking that whatever goes down will rise again. Chipping is not bottom fishing. Chippers want to buy into mutual funds that have been unfairly punished by the investing community. Since the timing of when investor's moods will change direction is unknown, assiduously follow rule three by buying a relatively small amount of a mutual fund to start and then buying more if its price goes down further as stated in rule four.

169

Rule five, should be modified to say "hold on to the fund until its price recovers most of the lost ground." Note how different this is than the rule for individual stocks. The reasons for this change are twofold. The first is institutional. Mutual funds punish investors who move in and out of funds. They try to dissuade Chipping type behavior. The second is that while individual stocks may never regain their lost price levels it is more likely that a fund will be able to do so once the market decides that this industry or country is once again on the buy list.

There is both an obvious advantage and disadvantage to Chipping mutual funds as compared to Chipping stocks. The advantage for novice traders is that it lets them invest in inefficient markets while the burden of stock picking can be offloaded to more professional hands. Along with this comes a reduction in risk as a result of the impact of diversification. The disadvantage is that it is harder to know when entire markets have become inefficiently priced than it is to know when a single stock has been too harshly punished. Finally, I don't know whether this is an advantage or a disadvantage: Chipping mutual fund is less exciting than Chipping stocks. Investors who crave excitement and have some experience trading should probably Chip stocks; less adventurous traders can learn and profit from mutual fund Chipping.

Examples

A five-year graph of the Fidelity Japan Fund is shown in Figure 1. Following its inception at $10 per unit in September 1992 the fund gradually rose from its offering price reaching a high of $15 in July 1994. Then sentiment turned against the Japanese economy and its markets fell. From $13.40 in August 1997 the fund fell to $8.90 in October 1998. That meant that Japanese stocks in the

170

aggregate were selling for about 1/3rd less than they had been fourteen months earlier. Yes, there economy was weak. Yes Japan has structural problems. I bought this fund because I felt that Japan was not going away (i.e., it was a great country) and that it would eventually resolve its fundamental issues. It took a while for the Japanese markets to recover but the fund exceeded $20 per unit (a 125% jump) by the end of December 1999 just fourteen months after it had hit bottom. Did I buy at the bottom? No, I Chipped the fund down from about $11 all the way to the bottom and then sold out before the top. But overall it was a fabulous investment.

Figure 1 Fidelity's Japan Fund
August 1993-October 2002

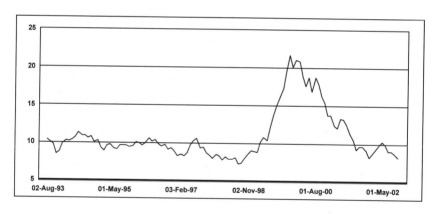

A second mutual fund Chipping opportunity is described in Figure 2 with the five-year trading history of the Fidelity Select Chemical Portfolio. The fund had risen fairly steadily from its inception in 1986 growing from $10 per unit to $45 by 1997. However, as the first quarter of 1998 came to an end, the stock market was roiled by several events including the Long-Term Capital debacle, a serious slow down in Asia, and a financial crisis in Russia.

The overall market fell by 18.5% from May to September of that year. Stock prices in the chemical industry were hit harder. By the end of the third quarter of 1998, the Chemical Portfolio had fallen by over 33%. Somehow Wall Street had decided that chemicals were done for. Were chemicals a great industry at that time? Yes of course. It is hard to imagine a world without chemicals. Did the mutual fund's price ever regain its lost ground? Yes, two and a third years later the price had fully recovered giving the investor nearly a 50% return.

CONCLUSION

Throughout this book, I have emphasized the distinction between day trading and Chipping. The idea of buying stocks and holding them for a short while before taking quick profits seems similar to the day-trading scheme of buying lots of stocks in one company and selling it minutes later but it is not. Chipping is not day trading. Likewise, Chipping mutual funds is not day trading either. But it also is not month trading or even quarter trading either. A typical mutual fund Chip is held for periods of a year or longer. Is it still worthwhile to Chip mutual funds? That depends on your level of success as you tryout the technique but above average rates of return are possible.

Figure 2 Fidelity's Select Chemical Portfolio
January 1997-October 2002

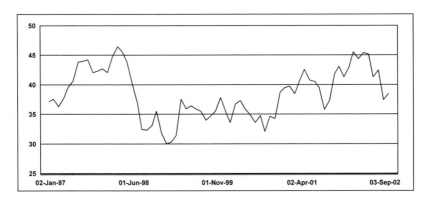

173

Chapter 8
The Nirvana of Chipping

For some investors, the stock market is a religion. That level of dedication is probably excessive. The religious analogue though runs throughout this concluding chapter because it describes so well the nearly spiritual transformation that devotees of the Chipping method strive to achieve. Investors can still profit without this conversion. But the conversion helps investors avoid unnecessary and potentially harmful regrets. Like the Joseph Kennedy maxim in Chapter 7, Chippers sell out too soon. They also get in too soon. Trading "misjudgments" are not peculiar to Chippers. They affect all investors. But Chipping encourages those errors with its blueprint for buying stocks after they fall precipitously and for selling them quickly when a nice profit is earned.

Chipping is not about making one big killing on the market; rather its goal is to make many small gains that over the course of time lead to major profits. Failure to buy at the bottom or sell at the top leads some investors to encourage self-recriminations that may frustrate their acceptance of this new way of trading. Converting the Chipping investor's beliefs to the new paradigm about stocks is the best way for him to avoid returning to other strategies like buy-and-hold, following the leader or day trading. Acquiescence to the total Chipping way is demanding and achieved gradually if at all. In addition to studying the steps to Nirvana that are laid out below readers should return to this Chapter whenever they fell guilty about taking a profit. It is incredibly difficult to not be affected when a stock is sold and then it keeps going up. They should keep constant track of their ascension up the Nirvana ladder in order to know their progress towards mastering the trading philosophy and modifying their investing behavior. The average investor will probably take

174

several years and hundreds of trades to approach the highest rung. Don't be hard on yourself if you never reach the goal. Few investors have the intellectual fortitude and mental focus to do so. Believe me, I am not permanently there myself.

I sincerely apologize in advance to anyone offended by my use of Buddhist imagery and the Nirvana phraseology. The American lexicon includes the notion of Nirvana as an ideal without a religious context. My intention is to use it solely for illustrative purposes and not to imply that any religion is concerned with trading activities or profit making.

THE STEPS TO REACHING CHIPPER'S NIRVANA

The Chipping trading philosophy is the antithesis of the traditional buy-and-hold dogma. Fundamental differences separate the two methods. Consider the comparisons in Table 1. While each of the differences is significant, the biggest difference between the two methods lie in the investor's proscribed continuing behavior. With the buy-and-hold method investors buy stocks and put them away while Chippers eagerly buy more when the price falls and enthusiastically take profits once the price rises.

Chipping's core principles differ from other trading techniques. That alone does not explain why a Chipper struggles to achieve a mental state of Nirvana. Other types of investors don't need affirmation. The explanation for the steps to Nirvana is that the Chipping investor constantly evaluates her trading success and invariably discovers "she should have done this or done that." In contrast, the buy-and-hold investor avoids that subject by the nature of his trading philosophy. If his stock's price should fall he says, "That's O.K. so long as the price recovers by the time I sell." If he eventually takes a profit he says, "See, the buy-and-hold method works." Chippers, on the other hand, evaluate their stock holdings daily deciding whether to buy more shares at lower prices or to take profits when prices rise. They buy and sell all the time. Curiosity and a need to refine their technique makes the Chipper look back and review if they should have held on longer before selling out or delayed the purchase or repurchase of a stock whose price fell.

Table 1 Differences between Buy-and-Hold and Chipping Investments

	Buy-and-hold	Chipping
Which stocks to buy	Companies doing well	Great companies whose prices fall after negative but not so bad news
When to sell	Not for a long time if ever	As soon as a good profit is earned and the stock appears to have stopped rising
Share holdings in one company	Virtually without limit	Never hold a large percentage of your portfolio in any one company
Behavior if the price falls after the initial purchase	Do nothing	Buy more
Behavior if the price rises after the initial purchase	Possibly buy more	Get ready to sell

The angst or self-doubt that inevitably afflicts Chippers takes on many forms as is described in Table 2. In each case, the Chipper should work to not castigate herself. Self-recrimination over failure to get the very highest price on stock sales or the very lowest price on purchases is a sign of wishful unrealistic thinking and a tendency to backstop to a buy-and-hold approach. It would be like if Ted Williams were angry with himself in 1941 when he batted .406. Sure he wanted to bat higher but no one has exceeded a .400 batting average in the seven decades since Williams' achievement. Making a 10% profit in a short while is like hitting .406 – a great accomplishment! The Chipper must learn to accept each trade's gains and not reflect on how much more she could have earned had she possessed a crystal ball. She needs to learn that no one always sells at the top and buys at the bottom. A Chipper needs to achieve a mental state wherein she understands the limitations and frailties of being human. These lessons move her towards Nirvana. As she climbs the ladder towards Nirvana the investor increases her chances of persevering with the method and not becoming a buy-and-hold or day-trading recidivist.

The steps to Nirvana begin slowly with the investor merely accepting the idea that Chipping may be an acceptable way to trade. Then gradually the steps intensify and bring the investor to the point where she is able to take quick profits and or buy stocks that fall further without feeling any remorse. In time, the investor may reach Chipping Nirvana.

Table 2 Expressions of a Chipper's Angst

Price Change After Purchase	Chipper's Behavior	Subsequent Price Movement	Expressions of Angst.
Rises	Sells	Keeps rising	"I should never have sold."
	Does nothing	Falls back	"I should have sold."
Falls	Buys more	Continues to fall	"I should never have bought more."
	Does nothing	Rises	"I should have bought."

Step 1 Make Your First Chip

Whether she is a novice stock trader or an experienced investor, the first task is to overcome a reluctance to try new things. Resistance to new ideas is part of human nature and is probably explained by our survival instinct. However, some investors need a change if their current trading method is not working (i.e., making a profit or leaving her better off than other investors). Chipping may be that alternative. For some investors it will be especially hard to give Chipping a try because the method requires the investor to abandon a system of beliefs that have been incessantly drummed into her by brokers and big investment firms. Chipping may help investors who have not profited from the "party line" espoused by big Wall Street firms. These are the most likely candidates to take the first step and do a Chip. Copying Neil Armstrong's lunar expression, this step is "One small step for the investor but one big step for his independence."

Making the first Chip is the hardest to do. For example, reviewing the July 8, 2002 newspaper you find a stock, JDA Software Inc. that fell by 44 percent, or $12 a share in the prior trading day to close at $15. The intra day low was $14. It was the leading percentage and net loss leader on the NASDAQ that day. The night before the company revealed that it expected to earn 17 to 18 cents a share for the second quarter on revenue of about $57 million. Analysts had expected a profit of 22 cents a share on revenue of $60.94 million. Would you be willing to buy a stock that fallen 44% in one day and hold it for a short while? Note that I chose this company as the illustration of a Chip by selecting a day at random (actually the day I was writing this section) on which to find a company to Chip. Had I wished, I could have carefully chosen from among thousands of other more profitable Chipping examples to find the case with the largest percentage return. But that would not have provided the reader with as unbiased an assessment of the technique.

Another interesting first Chip might be a stock like Royal Dutch Petroleum Company the international oil firm. On July 10, 2002 it slumped 9.2 percent, or $5.16, in a single day to $50.73, because the S&P 500 index dropped all foreign companies including Royal Dutch. Then several days later a former employee claimed that a tiny aspect of the company's accounting system was suspect. Within a week the stock was down over 17%. Nothing else had changed. Estimates of its future cash flows were untouched by the index's decision. It is true that markets were being pummeled that week by other accounting concerns but Royal Dutch's percentage decline exceeded by a factor of two the fall in the overall Dow Jones. A quick review of the company and its industry might easily lead to Royal Dutch being classified as great and being someone's first Chip. Could you have gotten up the nerve to buy a well-known stock that had fallen by 17% in 5 trading sessions?

Was JDA Software Inc. a bargain? After all it sold the next day for only 56% of the prior day's price. Its market capitalization fell from nearly $800 million to little more than $440 million. Is missing five cents a share for one quarter worth a $360 million markdown in value? Or is the company a fraud like WorldCom? A quick look with Yahoo Profiles reveals that JDA Software had nearly $76 million in cash and zero debt. Moreover, it is and has been profitable and has met analyst expectations throughout the difficult market of 2001 and early 2002. What do you do? Was this a single misstep that a finicky market overreacted to or is this the beginning of a slide to purgatory?

If you believe what you have read in this book and are willing to give it a try then buy a small amount of stock in a firm that you "discover" similar to JDA Software Inc. or Royal Dutch Petroleum Company and which you believe is a great company. But buy so little that if you lost the entire investment nothing in your life would need to change. Later larger purchases, though never excessive, are made if the great company stock falls further. Then watch the stock and sell it if its price partially rebounds. You've just achieved the first step toward Chipper's Nirvana.

Step 2 Buy More on a Price Drop

Suppose that step one was reached and an initial purchase was made. Then suppose that the price of the stock falls further. What do you do then? If you are a Chipper and believe that the further price reduction occurred because other investors panicked when they saw the initial price decline then you have another opportunity to buy the stock at an even greater discount. Before doing so double-check your great company calculations and reassure yourself that the company is really great. Often the second purchase follows a less frantic sell off allowing

180

more time to evaluate greatness. It may be reasonable to put an equal amount or slightly more money into the second purchase so that an even larger number of shares are acquired on the second buy.

Two days after the big fall in JDA Software Inc. described above the stock took a second hit. After rising to $15.50 on the very next day (a nice jump from the low of $14), the stock plunged to $11.31 after hitting a daily low of $10.89 apparently because a competitor, Retek Inc, issued cautions about its forthcoming quarter. How or why that "news" further affects JDA is a mystery but then the market is full of mysteries. Weakness in the overall market probably contributed to the decline too. Did the second fall reveal a fundamental weakness in the company or was the market simply over reacting?

Subsequent buys require ever more conviction that a company is truly great and not just a falling former great company. Generally your calculations will be on target since great companies are not "kind of great" or "will be great" if this or that happens, they are truly great companies. However, your vision will never penetrate a fraud such as occurred at WorldCom or Enron so keep the size of your investment in any one company small. In that case, even if hit by a scandal the shock to your account is small.

If as in the case of a company like JDA Software Inc. you make a subsequent purchase after the price falls still further, you have jumped onto the second wrung of the Nirvana ladder. That of course, does not guarantee profits or even break-even results from your investment. It does mean however that you have begun to modify your behavior in the ways of a Chipper.

181

Step 3 Take a Quick Profit

The third step to Nirvana is achieved by selling a stock purchased in step one after it achieves a modest 5 - 10% gain. Sounds easy. But wait until you try it. As you prepare to trade, competing thoughts pop into your head that involve holding on and making a bigger gain. You'll say things like, "if the stock is down 44% today maybe it will go back up $12 and I'll really make a killing." Maybe, but that's not Chipping. It's a form of bottom fishing combined with buy-and-hold investing. Take your profits and reach the third step to Nirvana.

Suppose you reached the first wrung on the Chipper's ladder by buying shares of JDA Software Inc. on July 5th, 2002 exactly between the daily low of $14 and the closing price of $15. Stock purchased for $14.50 could have been sold on the next trading day for as much as $16 or at the daily close of $15.50. The investor's profit was nearly 7% at the close and 10% at the intra day high. With three days passing between Friday the 5th and Monday the 8th, the investor's return on an annual basis at the closing price was 850%. Not to shabby an outcome. Had the investor missed out selling on the 8th because he was looking to earn more of the $12 price drop, he could also have sold the stock on August 22nd, for $15.75 at the high or $15.39 at the close. Using two months as the approximate holding period, the investor's annual return from $14.50 to $15.39 was 36%. Chippers know to keep a close watch over their portfolio. Because Chipping is not day trading they don't sit in front of a computer monitor all day and wait for a penny rise in a stock that signals that a sale can be made. But they do keep watch throughout the day. Getting a price quote every hour or so seems reasonable. Some services notify the investor when a stock makes a significant (defined by the investor) move. When its time to buy more or to sell out, frequent price quotes can save the investor some money.

A step two Chipper would have purchased more shares of JDA Software Inc. after its second price hit provided they still believed that it was a great company. Stock purchased at the close of trading on that second day, July 9th, 2002 for $11.31 could have been sold for a profit on the next day, $11.93 (nearly a 5.5% gain), or for still more on each of the next five day, and for as much as $15.39 per share seven weeks later. Of course, had the Chipper simply held on and waited for the stock to rebound to $27 per share where it started, she would have been sorely disappointed. As the NASDAQ market plunged in the summer of 2002 so too did JDA. Its stock hit a low of $5.94 on October 7th, 2002.

Step 4 Accept Profits with Grace

The fourth step to Chipper's Nirvana is reached when an investor who sells out in the third step feels no remorse after the stock's price keeps rising. Mentally this and the next step are difficult to achieve. Few investors are able to sell (buy) a stock too soon and not feel any pain. No one likes to leave money on the table. But a Step four Chipper knows not to look backwards. "A profit is a profit" as Gertrude Stein would say. Taking profits serves two purposes. First, it puts profits in the bank before they vanish in a market reversal. Second, it refreshes the investor' s pool of investable funds that is necessary for future investments.

Again JDA Software Inc. provides an interesting case in point. If the investor had sold out all of her shares on July 10th, 2002 for $11.93 after having bought it the day before for $11.31 she would have earned profits at an annual rate of 2,000% per annum. Despite this fabulous success consider the investor's remorse when JDA's price hit $15.39 about seven weeks later. I've been there. The feeling is terrible and the self-doubt and frustration with Chipping is palpable. But when would she have sold the stock? If she fell back into the buy-and-hold philosophy she would not have sold out at $15.39 either. I suppose she would have still held the stock at $5.94 on October 7th, 2002.

After a stock is sold, sometimes the price falls, other times it rises.

On average it probably does nothing. If it always rises after a sale the investor is selling too soon and needs to recalibrate her behavior. Investors should never evaluate their Chipping skills based on just one or even a few trades. Get a sense of how well you are Chipping by averaging over returns over a number of trades. If after a sale the price keeps rising don't feel bad just count your profits.

Step 5 Accept Losses with Equanimity

The next step to Chipper's Nirvana is accomplished when the investor is able to suppress angst that comes from buying shares too soon after a major price drop, for example day one in the JDA Software Inc. example above, or making a follow-up purchase too soon after a second price fall. Self-doubt overwhelms investors when they make that mistake. Step five Chippers know that they cannot always be right and that it is impossible to predict the bottom. Yet they also know that a purchase or an additional purchase of a great company's stock at a still lower price usually works out when its price recovers. Afterward the mistake, assuming that the price has stabilized, the Chipper becomes a holder waiting for the stock to pop back up.

Chipping is not buying stocks that have merely dipped a little. Look for major declines in price: 20, 30 or even 50%. Don't get sucked into buying a stock too early

184

following a paltry dip. Wait for great stocks to take a big hit. Chippers are looking to buy great company stocks that fallen a lot after a not so bad announcement.

Step 6 A Missed Selling Opportunity Causes More Angst than Selling out Too Soon

Chipping Nirvana's sixth step is achieved when the investor feels worse having missed an opportunity to sell out at a profit than when shares are sold too soon. Suppose a purchase is made at $10 per share and then the price rises to $11. The investor on the sixth step to Nirvana feels worse if the price subsequently falls back to $10 without having sold out than if after selling the stock the price rises still further to $12. Both events cost the investor $1 but it is the failure to behave as a proper Chipper that leads to the first loss while the second loss is due to uncontrollable events that have pushed the price up still further. The movement towards Nirvana matches the investor's behavioral movement towards the idealized Chipping model.

An investor not yet on the sixth rung may feel equal pain from either $1 loss. More likely, he may be bothered more by the rise to $12 a share than the fall back to $10 because in his mind he still owns the $10 stock and can sell it in the future. The Chipper knows that had he sold at $11 he might have repurchased the shares at $10 and then he too could resell them again at some point in the future.

Step 7 Ascending to Nirvana

Nirvana occurs when an investor adopts all of the positive and negative precepts of the Chipping methodology and overcomes emotional, intellectual, and historic resistance to those ideas. The precepts are listed in Table 3.

Have I ascended to the top of the ladder? That certainly is a fair question. I suppose that the answer is yes and no. There are times when I feel totally a Chipper but then doubts gradually creep in and push me down a rung or two. When that happens I work hard to get back to Chipping's core principles.

Good luck as you investment. Keep evaluating your skills and modifying your behavior to accentuate your strengths and avoid your weaknesses. If you are good at Chipping then keep doing it. If not, find some other way to put your money to work.

Table 3 The Precepts of Chipping

Positive Precepts

Only buy stock in great companies.

Wait to buy until the price of the great company is beaten down on a single day for a not so important reason.

If the price falls significantly again soon for no apparent reason then buy more shares.

Constantly reassesses the great company designation.

If the price rises significantly sell out.

Hold plenty of cash always!

Keep your investment in a single company to a reasonable small number of dollars.

Invest gradually in different companies compiling a portfolio of great companies.

If a stock has been purchased more than once, when it comes to taking profits treat each purchase separately.

If a great company goes bad take your losses before the price hits zero and get out.

Negative Precepts

Don't buy hyped or touted companies.

Don't buy stock when the price falls gradually over a number of days.

Don't buy more shares if the price falls just a bit or goes up somewhat.

Don't get stuck with a great company that goes sour.

Don't get caught thinking the price will recover to its old level.

Don't think the market has bottomed even after all the experts claim that it has.

Don't put all your eggs in one basket.

Don't put all your money to work on the same day.

Don't let a good profit on a second trade become a loss by waiting until the price rises enough for all shares to be profitable.

Don't hope for miracles.

Epilogue

October 2, 2002

WHAT A YEAR IT WAS!

I began to write *Chipping: The New Stock Market Method for Surviving Turbulence and Hitting a Hole-in-One* in early 2001. The market had already begun to decline but the terrorist attack of September 11, 2001, the onslaught of accounting scandals in major American firms, and evidence that the telecom sector was caught in a depression had not yet surfaced. As my pen hit the paper it seemed that the country was merely in another of a long string of recessions dating back to colonial times whose resolution would require the normal nine to fifteen months before growth would resume. The Federal Reserve and its chairman Alan Greenspan seemed to be on the same page as they accommodated the recovery with eleven consecutive interest rate cuts that pushed rates to levels not seen in recent memory. Moreover, Congress' spendthrift ways learned during the years of budget surpluses promised continued Federal and State spending to further accommodate the impending recovery.

How wrong I was! Yes interest rates plunged throughout 2001 and early in 2002. The prime rate fell to 4.75% and the discount rate to an unbelievable 1.25% but economic activity dragged into a recovery that lacked a burst of new job creation. Consumer confidence shaken by terrorism remained low and beyond the housing sector, consumer spending remained constrained. The telecom depression spread to sectors supplying that industry like a string of dominoes. And most damaging of all, accounting scandals sapped investor confidence in financial markets

188

and in the veracity of accounting reports. The SECs mandate that CEOs of large companies sign and take personal responsibility for financial statements commencing with the 2nd quarter of 2002 may prove to be a sufficient remedy for investor skepticism.

From the market's peak to the bottom in October 2002 (my guess may prove wrong), investors lost more than $7 trillion out of $17 trillion dollars of equity value in American financial markets. Still worse they lost confidence in the buy-and-hold investing system that Wall Street had promulgated as the right course. That model may still function for pension fund investments managed by external firms when the investor does not expect to see the money for 20 or 30 years. But in my opinion it fails miserably for regular investing. Ask the people who gave back the $7 trillion.

HOW WELL DID I FARE?

How well did Chipping do in these turbulent times? Overall my batting average was probably better than most investors but in certain investments it was worse. In part my superior results came from following the rules to limit the investment in any one firm and to keep most funds in cash. My failings were in the great company classification area. I bought WorldCom at $9 and sold at $10, bought again at $4.75 and sold at $6.15, but then bought it down to $1.72 just before it collapsed. I failed to sell out at $2 before the revelations (greed got to me) and could only sellout later at $0.24 thereby taking a bath. I also believed that several telecom suppliers like Ciena Corporation and Juniper Systems were great companies servicing a growing and necessary sector. Apparently I was wrong! I believe that these investments will eventually pay off because of patience and continued downside buying. But I wouldn't wish my experiences with them onto my worst enemy.

I still believe strongly in the Chipping method. Companies worth $30 a share one day shouldn't fall to $15 a share on the next day when their CEO announces that he is getting divorced or that earnings will miss the target of some supposed expert by one cent. Just this week, Walgreen Company fell from $35 to $30 in a day because analyst had expected them to earn $0.25 per share for the quarter and it only earned $0.24 versus last year's $0.21. It accomplished this in a weak and flagging economy. I don't know Walgreen's future price but it was certainly in my mind a perfect example of a Chipping candidate.

My major failing was in succumbing to the mistake of letting the fact that a company once traded at $90 a share have an impact on my assessment of its true greatness. It should not. Most of my "regular" Chips worked even throughout this turbulent period; unfortunately, most of my high-technology Chips did not. Chipping cannot hold back the tide. When the market collapses all investor fall with it except for short sellers.

I realize that not everyone is suited to the discipline and attention demands of Chipping. Yet I believe that the technique will benefit many investors both directly (as they ascend the Chipping Nirvana ladder) and indirectly (as they modify their trading behavior).

Appendix A
Examples of Successful Chips

Show me! That's what everybody always asks when thinking about something new whether it is a car, a new job, or a new way to trade stocks. Examples of how I have personally Chipped stocks are given below. Keep in mind that not every Chip works out. Sometimes your great company call is wrong and you need to exit as soon as possible. Success is more likely when the market is rising, flat or at least not falling precipitously. The old adage "don't fight the tape" is true. If the marker is in a free-fall don't Chip and don't invest; just sit on the sidelines. When reviewing these examples be aware that historical results are not an indication of how successful you will be in the future.

Chips are classified into three categories.
- One shot pops
- Saved by additional purchase(s)
- Not so great companies

Several examples are presented below in each category. Arguably some of the companies were not great. I admit that. My excuse is that I got too involved with proving to myself that the Chipping method works and too convinced of my own expertise and began to Chip some not so great companies. I hope that I have learned my lesson: stick with only great companies. Even then some of the companies will turn out to be not so great. I provide the actual trading prices.

Many of these trades came during months of turbulent market activity. Obviously, like other trading methods Chipping has risks too. Perhaps the most important factor leading to Chipping success is the selection of "great" companies: be careful and deliberate in that choice. Much of its power rests in the investor's ability to choose great

191

companies. Frequently, the trades described below took place at better prices than the daily closing prices for those securities. When buying a Chip I try to wait until panicked sellers have set a low and when selling I try to catch the end of the buyer's euphoria. Obviously, I have made many mistakes in both the choice of great companies and in the buying/selling timing. The graphs provide additional data covering the period before the purchase and after the sale. This allows the reader to see that in all cases the prices fell dramatically before I purchased and that very often the price continued to rise after I sold out. I try not to let the later bother me as I work my way up the Nirvana ladder.

ONE SHOT POPS

Invitrogen Corporation - IVGN

| 03/01/2002 | 40 | $32.19 | $1,287.60 |
| 03/06/2002 | -40 | $36.98 | ($1,479.20) |

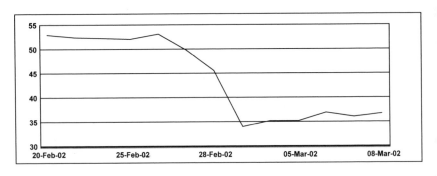

Kensey Nash Corporation - KNSY

| 03/15/2002 | 100 | $16.29 | $1,629.00 |
| 04/11/2002 | -100 | $18.47 | ($1,847.10) |

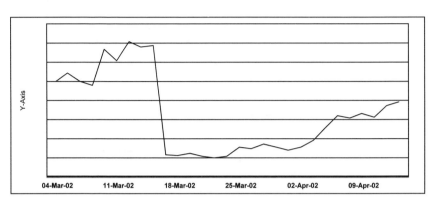

McDATA Corporation - MCDTA

| 04/24/2002 | 180 | $6.20 | $1,115.82 |
| 05/01/2002 | -180 | $6.60 | ($1,188.18) |

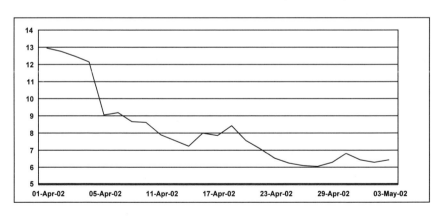

MSC.Software Corp. -MNS

| 04/22/2002 | 100 | $10.87 | $1,087.00 |
| 04/23/2002 | -100 | $12.06 | ($1,206.00) |

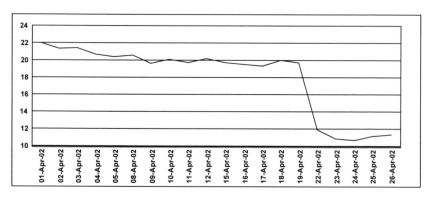

Macrovision Corporation -MVSN

| 10/30/2001 | 55 | $25.04 | $1,377.20 |
| 11/06/2001 | -55 | $28.51 | ($1,568.05) |

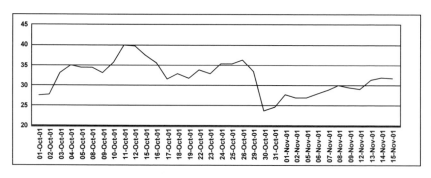

Oakley, Inc. - OO

| 02/23/2001 | 100 | $14.41 | $1,441.00 |
| 02/26/2001 | -100 | $17.03 | ($1,703.00) |

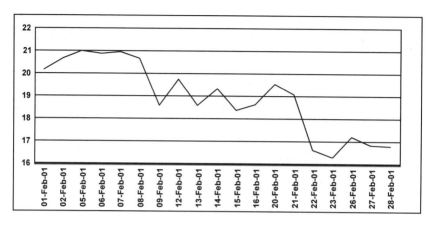

Palm, Inc - PALM

| 05/24/2000 | 50 | $20.69 | $1,034.38 |
| 05/31/2000 | -50 | $23.69 | ($1,184.38) |

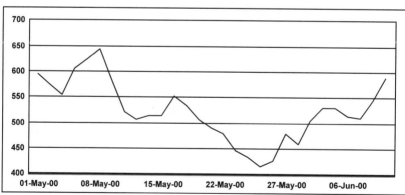

Prices in the graph are split adjusted.

PerkinElmer, Inc. –PKI

03/01/2002	100	$15.93	$1,593.00
03/26/2002	-100	$17.58	($1,758.00)

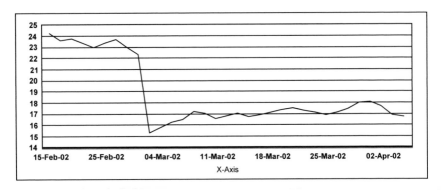

The Boston Beer Company, Inc., - SAM

02/27/2002	100	$12.15	$1,215.00
03/06/2002	-100	$14.02	($1,402.00)

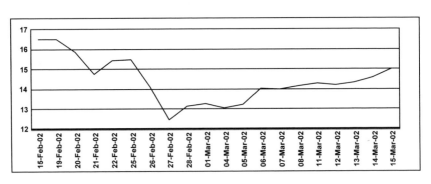

Xcel Energy Inc - XEL

07/26/2002	200	$8.05	$1,610
08/12/2002	-200	$10.16	($2,032.00)

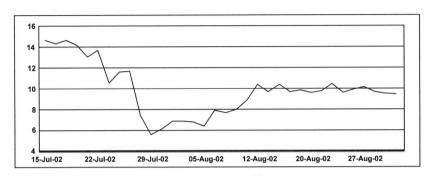

SAVED BY ADDITIONAL PURCHASE(S)

BioSource International Inc - BIOI

05/21/2001	300	$7.30	$2,190.00
07/28/2001	300	$6.40	$1,920.00
10/30/2001	-300	$7.04	($2,112.00)
11/13/2001	-300	$7.56	($2,268.00)

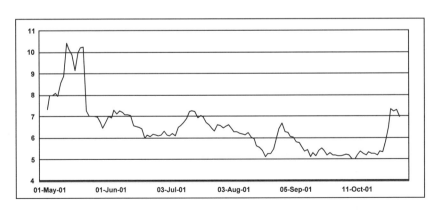

E-Trade Group Inc. – ET

03/01/2001	100	$8.93	$893.00
03/12/2001	150	$7.56	$1,134.00
04/12/2001	-250	$8.53	($2,132.50)

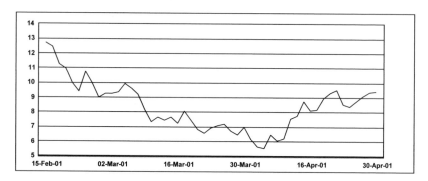

Oracle Inc - ORCL

03/02/2001	75	$16.75	$1,256.25
03/12/2001	80	$15.25	$1,220.00
04/16/2001	-80	$16.15	($1,292.00)
04/18/2001	-75	$18.71	($1,403.25)

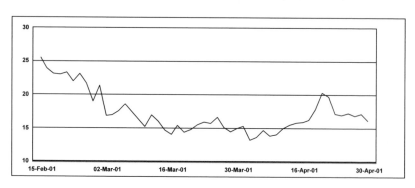

Six Flags, Inc - PKS

08/14/2002	200	$5.05	$1,010.00
10/02/2002	300	$3.44	$1,032.00
11/01/2002	-500	$4.60	($2,300.00)

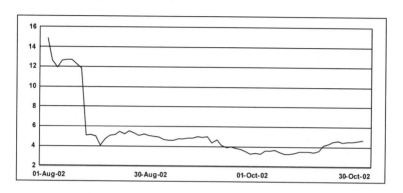

PMC-Sierra, Inc.– PMCS

02/27/2001	30	$41.00	$1,230.00
02/28/2001	30	$37.94	$1,138.13
03/12/2001	40	$33.44	$1,337.50
04/18/2001	-70	$33.04	($2,312.80)
04/20/2001	-30	$45.01	($1,350.30)

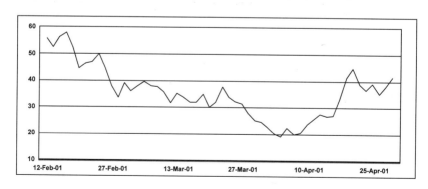

NOT SO GREAT COMPANIES

WorldCom Inc – WCOM

01/30/2002	150	$9.03	$1,354.35
01/31/2002	-150	$9.99	($1,498.65)
02/15/2002	225	$6.68	$1,503.00
04/11/2002	275	$4.76	$1,308.73
04/16/2002	-275	$6.15	($1,691.25)
04/22/2002	300	$4.00	$1,200
04/23/2002	400	$3.44	$1,376
05/06/2002	700	$1.83	$1,281.00
05/08/2002	-700	$2.30	($1,610.00)
05/10/2002	750	$1.72	$1,290.00
07/03/2002	-1675	$0.24	($402.00)
	1675		$4,513.18

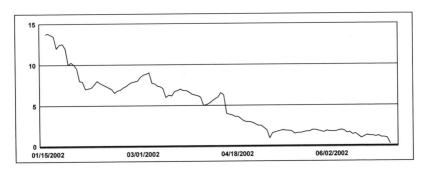

The company was delisted from the stock exchange; consequently, the graph above is approximate and is for illustration purposes only.

Appendix B
Using Yahoo: Finding Opportunities in the Detritus

Yahoo! Finance is an invaluable research tool in the search for great companies whose stock prices have tumbled for relatively minor reasons. The three questions that I ask daily and how I use Yahoo! Finance to watch the market and look for Chipping opportunities are described below.

HOW IS THE MARKET DOING?

My Internet home page starts at Yahoo! Finance. On it are displayed a real time quote of the overall market, the Dow Jones Industrials (DJ INDU AVERAGE (CBT:^DJI) and the NASDAQ composite (NasdaqSC:^IXIC). Also displayed are 20 minute delayed price quotes of stocks that I either own or am watching closely.

WHICH STOCKS ARE DOWN THE MOST?

Early and late each day I try to visit a Yahoo! Finance page that displays the day's largest percentage price changes. The current URL is (http://finance.yahoo.com/mnpl?e=NQ). All three major markets are displayed at this site. If one of the stocks seems like a possible Chip, by clicking on its name Yahoo! sends me to a page that displays a delayed quote for it, news items and other valuable information about the company.

IS IT A GREAT COMPANY?

This is the hardest question of all. In search of an answer, I examine the company's data displayed on the Profile page for that stock symbol in Yahoo! Finance. Some of the questions I ask are:

    a. Are the company's executives over paid?
    b. Does the company have plenty of cash?
    c. Does the company have too much debt?
    d. Is its price too high given its level of sales?
    e. Is its price too high given its level of profits?
    f. Does the company earn a profit?

Further details for the company are uncovered in the *"More Information"* tab that provides:

    Quotes and Charts (for one day, five days, three months, six months, one year, two years, five years and maximum data.
    News both current and historic
    Research information from analyst provided not by individual but as aggregates
    Insider Trading Data
    Financials: Income Statement, Balance Sheet, and Cash Flow Statement

In the epilogue I talked about the sharp decline in Walgreen's stock price that took place during the last week of September and into the first week of October 2002. Here's what a quick look at Yahoo!Finance and the Profile section reveals about Walgreens.:

- The CEO is paid $2.5 million per year. A huge sum but actually relatively low for a firm with $29 billion in sales.

- Cash is a healthy $286 million.
- The company has no debt.
- Profits are positive, with a net profit margin to sales of 3.6% and a return on equity of 18.2%.
- The price is high relative to earnings at about a 32 multiple.
- The price is moderate relative to sales at a ratio of about 1.14 to 1.
- The stock price high for the year was about $41 per share and the low was $30.
- The research section reveals that analyst anticipate further growth next year.

All in all, the company looked like a pretty good Chip to me.

The Profile page contains far more information on this and other companies. Some readers will find that to be of further help.

Appendix C:
Keeping Track of What You're Doing

Like the hardware storeowner, a Chipper must keep close track of what stocks he owns and how much he paid for them. This vital information is necessary when it comes time to sell stocks, buy stocks and pay income taxes. I use a spreadsheet that looks like this:

Keeping this spreadsheet handy is helpful when the price of XYZ Inc. pops to $12.95. It helps answer the question should I sell the last shares purchased, all of my shares, or none of the shares? Similarly, if the price falls to $9.99 and I still think the company is great it helps me to decide how many more shares I want to buy.

XYZ Inc.

Company Name	Date Purchased	Number of Shares	Price Paid	Dollars	Average Price
XYZ Inc.	1/1/01	100	$13.45	$1345.00	
	2/1/01	150	$11.85	$1725.00	
Total		250		$3070.00	$12.28